The Bedfordshire Family of Laces

TO BRIAN AND KATHY

First published in 1991 by Kangaroo Press Pty Ltd
3 Whitehall Road (P.O. Box 75) Kenthurst 2156
Typeset by G.T. Setters Pty Limited
Printed in Hong Kong by Colorcraft Ltd

ISBN 0 86417 328 8

Contents

The mat 'Venus', with a looped picot edge (page 38)

The Bedfordshire Family of Laces

Jennifer Fisher

Kangaroo Press

Foreword

Maltese. . .Cluny. . .Bedfordshire. . .names familiar not only to most lacemakers, but also to many members of the general public, partly due to the comparatively large quantities of antique laces of these styles which are to be found in *many* countries world-wide, and partly due to the ease with which excellent reproductions, most of which are just called 'Cluny lace', can be produced on machines. The three 'real' laces which comprise this family of lace are all very similar, both in the way they are worked and in their appearance, having, as we shall see, a single parent, but each lace has its own personality and idiosyncrasies.

To date, each lace has been treated separately in publications, but with the new global view of lace which is developing—with, for example, Dutch lacemakers becoming expert in Honiton lacemaking, English lacemakers writing books on traditional European laces—it is much more appropriate to take a broader view of lace than a specialist one. In the newer countries lace-wise, such as the United States, Australia and New Zealand, we have no traditional laces which we can claim as our own heritage and thus we find most laces being made, sometimes with little knowledge of the precise characteristics of many of them, which I find rather sad.

I cannot conclude this foreword without expressing my thanks to a good many people who have assisted me in so many ways in the preparation of this work. To Dorothy Barton, Pat Morris and Betty Williams, who have each worked large parts of the manuscript; to Kerry Dowling who took the black and white photographs, and to Kathy Griffith who once again assisted with the colour plates. To Margaret Hamer who introduced me to Bedfordshire lace and has given valuable advice regarding this text, and to Josephine Caruana who checked, and corrected, my self-taught Maltese techniques, and gave me permission to use her Maltese Cross pattern and christening gown. To Marion, Liz, Pam, Norma, Linda and Denise, who constantly gave help and support in a variety of ways, and finally to my 'second family' at Little Bay without whose help and encouragement this book would not have been completed.

Introduction

Before starting to make the three laces from the family with which we are currently concerned—Maltese, Bedfordshire-Maltese and Cluny—let's take a brief look at each in turn.

All three laces are direct descendants of the Italian Genoese lace, but the English version, the Bedfordshire-Maltese lace, is once removed. They are of the broader family of lace known as straight guipure laces, meaning that the lace is made as a complete piece, with the main pattern features being joined as they are worked. The majority of these links are either plaited bars, sometimes with picots, sometimes without, or tallies. Towards the end of the book we will be using some of the fillings found in Bedfordshire lace as grounds, but in the main these are borrowed from other English laces. It can be very confusing, as the plaits and tallies are called by different names in each of these three laces. Suffice it at this stage to give an example—further detail will be given as the appropriate stage is met—but Bedfordshire workers still call a plait a 'leg' and a tally a 'plait'.

Of these three laces, Maltese is probably the oldest, but the earliest laces made on the islands differed considerably from the Maltese lace we know today. In the early sixteenth century, at the time of the Turkish siege against Malta, a Maltese nobleman went to Spain where he learnt how to make Spanish lace, which at this time was largely made from gold and silver and, to a lesser degree, black thread. On his return to Malta, he taught his three sisters how to make this lace, and thus began the first Maltese lace industry. However, as with many early industries, the art of

lacemaking fell into decay, and it was not until 1833 that the second period in the history of Maltese lacemaking began. In that year, Lady Hamilton Chichester introduced lacemakers from Genoa to teach the Maltese how to make lace, largely for commercial purposes, and in particular for the tourist trade. It was for this reason that the Maltese Cross was introduced into most pieces of lace, a tradition which continues in large measure today.

Cluny lace, the French representative of this family of laces, first appeared in France in the nineteenth century, and was based on the sixteenth century laces in the Musée d'Antiquities, then housed in the Hotel de Cluny in Paris. It is, however, also an offshoot of the Genoese laces and its origin is debated, some saying that this style of lace reached the French lacemakers, especially in the Auvergne region of France, via the East Midlands counties of England—which, don't forget, had already adapted the Maltese lace to their own needs—while others claim a direct descent from Genoa. Whatever its origins, the making of Cluny lace was added to the repertoire of the lacemakers of the Auvergne, especially in the Le Puy area, where there was a sizeable lace industry at the time, it being estimated that around 200 000 peasant folk supplemented the meagre incomes obtained largely from hill farming by selling their lace, which found its way to many European countries.

One of the main strengths of the Le Puy lace industry has been the makers' ability to keep up with the dictates of fashion; in this way, gold and silver laces gave way to the guipure lace, largely made in black silk imported from Barcelona (Spain) at one stage, and later to the now well-known biscuit-coloured silk, almost a cross between cream, broken white and ecru as we variously know the colours of lacemaking threads today. In the eighteenth century, fashion dictated a much more delicate lace, with a fine ground. One can imagine the distress with which the lacemakers, then making largely guipure lace which was comparatively quick and easy to make, rendering a reasonable profit, greeted this fashion, the new lace taking longer to make and thus reducing their profits considerably.

Bedfordshire-Maltese lace, as it was then known, first appeared on the scene in the 1840s, probably having been introduced to this East Midlands county which had previously shared the point ground tradition with its neighbouring counties, Buckinghamshire, and—to a lesser degree—Northamptonshire, by either migrants or travellers.

The Bedfordshire workers found that they could make the guipure lace much more quickly than their traditional laces, and again, could increase their profits, but the change to this type of lace was frowned on by their traditional neighbours, who considered guipure lace to be very inferior to the finer point ground, and who also decried the ease with which errors could be covered up, in direct contrast to the same features in the point ground lace. However, guipure lace of the Maltese-Le Puy varieties was in Bedfordshire to stay and in due time Maltese was generally dropped from the name—but not entirely—and this form of bobbin lace became known as Bedfordshire lace, and developed some of its own characteristics which we will be exploring together during the course of this book. Today, as Margaret Hamer so correctly pointed out in an article in *Lace*, the quarterly journal of the Lace Guild (UK), there is a tendency for these traditional features to be lost with 'the constant exchange of patterns with those of other countries, through books and through travel' (*Lace*, 38, p.31). Neither she nor I has any objection to the 'muddling up' of these three—and occasionally other—styles of lace, as long as the resulting piece of lace is not incorrectly labelled Bedfordshire or Cluny when the individual features belong strictly to one lace or the other. The tallies we meet in Chapter 2 are probably the best illustration of this point that one could find.

I could not leave these few words about Bedfordshire lace without mentioning the man who was probably the greatest exponent of Bedfordshire lace of all time. Thomas Lester was a lace merchant, designer and maker of Bedford, and he took Bedfordshire lace and turned it into the earliest art form of the East Midlands, using themes from nature as the basis of his designs. As well as using, in the main, his native Bedfordshire lace to work his exquisite designs, he was not afraid to borrow techniques from other laces to add to the richness of his lace. A large collection of his lace can now be seen in the Cecil Higgins Museum, Bedford—but beware, overseas visitors, their opening hours are not exactly 'normal'! Do check before you make a special trip to Bedford.

About this book

This is not a book for raw beginners in the art of lacemaking, and therefore the book is designed slightly differently from my other two. Most chapters contain three pieces of lace related to the topic which is named in the chapter headings; a few chapters have only two pieces of lace in them. It was my aim to include in each chapter one piece of lace which is easier than the other two, one of medium difficulty, and one which will give each lacemaker a real challenge. The instructions and diagrams in the first few pieces are reasonably full to ensure a sound knowledge of the basic techniques; thereafter they gradually become thinner, until in the last couple of chapters only the barest minimum of working notes are given.

While I have not made direct suggestions on the suitability of each piece of work for a finished article, I have often included a few ideas. Some of my readers will choose to make samples for a working notebook, but I do urge you to work at least every third to fourth piece of lace so that it can be *used*; I say this for two main reasons. Firstly, it is only after you have worked a goodly number of pattern repeats that you can stop thinking of the techniques and start thinking about making lace! Secondly, I am sure that most people get great satisfaction from wearing or using or seeing their own lace, and I cannot believe that a book full of samples gives the same pleasure as the finished article, whether made all of lace or trimmed with lace.

On the other hand, of course, there are many lacemakers who will have nothing to do with samples who, if they wish to do an assessment or exam, must use the false method of working the samples *after* the work has been done—surely the wrong way around? You just cannot win! I get around this problem by using my rough working samples as just that, making it quite clear that these are what are being looked at—not the perfectly finished piece of lace.

Before we start

If there are still any readers who have only a little knowledge of another lace—usually either torchon or braid lace—you should refer to your original textbook if one was used, and revise as much as possible of it, in particular any points which you have forgotten. Here a good working knowledge of the basic techniques used in bobbin lace is assumed and I will not be describing any of the following:

> *whole stitch* (often abbreviated to wh. st.)
> *half stitch* (occasionally 1/2 st.)
> *double stitch* or (wh. st.; twist)
> *basic footside edge* (straight edge), and the footside using a torchon join
> *plaits*—with and without picots; *single* and *double* picots
> *tallies*
> *starting and finishing* a piece of lace
> *adding in pairs (prs)* and *taking or throwing out prs* while the work is in progress
> *taking a sewing*

The following terminology, which has been used in my two earlier books, should be noted:

> *changeover stitch*: wh. st. and 2–3 twists, worked on the outer edge of the footside (also known as the straight edge)

bobbins hung in V-formation: bobbins hung in pairs (see figure below).
workers: weavers

Bobbins hung in V-formation   Bobbins hung in pairs

Materials you will need to work the lace in this book

• 1–2 lace pillows—the second is always useful if you 'haven't quite finished' a long length, but feel the need to try something fresh as well as continuing with the first piece of lace. Working cloths and cover cloths for the pillow(s).

• 85 pairs of bobbins (minimum)

• Thread—Nos. 35–40; 60; 80 and 100 linen lace thread; the cotton or silk equivalents to at least some of these thread sizes—see Appendix 1, p.141. You will find it much more interesting to work in a variety of threads, but it is easiest to name the linen threads and then take the equivalents from them.

• pins—both medium (approximately 1 1/16 × 026) and fine. The former are used for threads sized 80 or coarser, unless you want to make a feature of the pin holes, when they can be used for any of the above-mentioned threads. The fine pins are used for thread sized 80 (linen) and finer. It is very important to use the correct sized pins if you are to get an even tension on the edge of the lace, and also if the picots or snatch pin loops are to be appropriate in size to the rest of the lace.

• pricker; pricking pad; pricking card; 'old' scissors for cutting the card

• fine sharp scissors; crochet hook sized 0.60; divider or hat pins

• any other favourite accessory of your own.

Abbreviations

wh. st. = whole (or cloth, or linen) stitch
1/2 st. = half or lattice or torchon stitch
pr = pair
fig. = figure
l. = left (l.h. side); r. = right
cm = centimetre
prs = pairs
ch(s) = chapters

Markings on Diagrams
②= 2 prs to be hung on
(+1) = 1 pr to be added in; (−2) = 2 prs to be thrown out
╪= 1 twist; ╫ = 2 twist, etc.

1 Plaits—or legs—and picots

Plaits are a very important part of all guipure style laces, but especially of Cluny and Bedfordshire laces—in fact, these laces are sometimes referred to as plaited laces. Maltese lace, however, does not use plaits in the same way as the other two, and the various parts of this style of lace are more likely to be joined by petal-shaped tallies or simple twisted bars. To add to the confusion that often arises when using different techniques, traditionally in Bedfordshire a plait is referred to as a 'leg'!

Plaits are simple to make and quick to execute, but not always easy to fit into a given space or to get perfectly even. If you have never worked a plait before you are strongly recommended to make a practice one before embarking on your first piece of lace—even this can be used for a gift tie or a tie belt for a dress if you choose appropriate thread or cord!

The two edgings given make very suitable borders for handkerchiefs, while the insertion can be put to a variety of uses, from trimming for a lampshade to an insertion down the sleeves of a blouse.

Kirribilli

Materials: 16 prs of bobbins wound in No. 60 linen lace thread, or the equivalent cotton thread (see Appendix 1, page 141). Materials for making a pricking. Fabric for mounting the finished lace.

Preparation: Decide on your finished article; wind the bobbins accordingly—for example, if planning to make a 12 cm square handkerchief edging you are advised to wind your bobbins full, but not over-full, or the knot will constantly slip. The thread on the neck ('long neck' to some lacemakers) should not extend beyond the line of the shank. Make your pricking from the pattern in Pricking 1.

If necessary, work a practice plait.

Take two prs of bobbins and wind them with a fairly heavy thread, No. 5 or No. 8 pearl, for example. Knot the ends with an overhand knot and pin to the pillow through this knot. *Work one or two half stitches, then, holding each bobbin separately between your fingers—i.e. bobbins 2 and 3 (numbered in the normal way from l. to r.) between the thumb and forefinger, and nos. 1 and 4 between fingers 3 and 4 on each hand—ease the threads up into position ** Repeat from * to ** as often as needed, pinning between the two prs. every 5 cm.

Yes, it sounds simple, but care needs to be

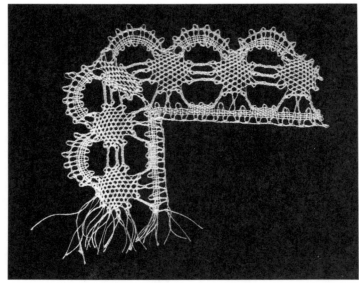

Plate I The corner of 'Kirribilli'

Fig. 1.1 A half-stitch plait

taken. The plait should be perfectly even; it must not be too loose—if so it looks sloppy—or too tight—if so it looks knobbly! Newcomers to plaits sometimes find it beneficial to ease the threads up between each half stitch until they have the feel of it. Continue until you are *quite* happy with the result or you reach the desired length; remove from the pillow and knot the end with an overhand knot to match the start.

To Work

1. Following the working diagram, Fig. 1.2, hang 2 prs of workers around pin A, in V formation. Make an additional pin hole in the footside between A and C; hang 2 prs of passives from this pin, and 2 prs around pin C. Work plain footside to C including the 2 prs hanging on this pin. Take out pin C and replace under the twisted workers; work back to the footside edge, and

12

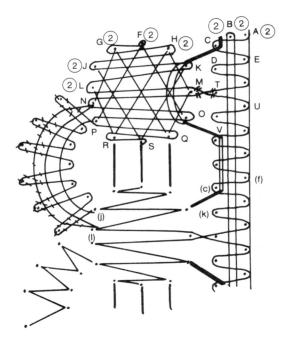

Fig. 1.2 Working diagram for the edging 'Kirribilli'

work the changeover stitch. Continue the footside to E, leaving out 2 prs at C. Note that nothing comes into or goes out from pin D: this is called a *snatch pin*.

2. Work a plait from C to K, carefully watching the length; it should be slightly shorter than the distance between these 2 pins to allow room for the stitch and pin at K. You may like to put up a temporary pin in K between the two prs, but there is no need to do so.

3. Now start the half stitch circle, called a 'bud'. You may like to hang all the prs on their respective pins before starting, or you may prefer to add in the prs as you reach the pin; the former prevents prs being missed while the latter gives more room for careful easing up, especially at the ends of rows where new prs have been added, and where there is a tendency for these prs to creep away from the pins leaving an ugly gap. All prs are hung in V-formation. Whichever method you choose, start at F with 2 new prs. Cover the pin with a (wh. st.; twist each pr once) and then bring in 2 new prs at G, working the first pr half stitch and

the edge pr (wh. st.; twist; 1–2 extra twists to the workers; take out the pin, and replace under the twisted workers (the lace will not fall apart, as the 'new' threads lie on the workers!); wh. st.; twist).

Work in half stitch to H; bring in 2 new prs as at G; continue with the bud in half stitch, with the (wh. st.; twist) before and after each pin. At K the prs from the plait are added in, in the same manner as new prs are added. The final two prs are added at L.

4. At M link the workers of the bud with those of the footside by means of a kiss. Bring the bud workers to M; twist 2–3 times as usual; put up a pin in M.

Turn to the footside and bring those workers through to T; twist; pin.

Cross the workers with a (wh. st.; 2–3 twists—whichever you used for pins M and T). Note that there is no pin.

Allow the 2 prs of workers to pass below their respective pins; take the footside workers out to U; work the changeover stitch, and leave.

Take the bud workers and complete the bud, leaving out 2 prs at each of the pins N, O, P, Q, R and S. Remember that it is 2 prs of passives which are left out, not the workers, and that you continue to work (wh. st., and twist) before and after each pin; the 2 prs left out will be the edge pr and the last half st. pr.

5. Work plaits with each of the 2 prs left out at O, Q, R and S.

6. Return to the footside and work to (f), noting that you will have 2 extra prs of passives between (V) and (c). These 2 prs are left out at (c) to work the plait to (k).

The headside

7. This is a basic scallop, with 3 prs of passives, a twisted edge and one pr of workers. The 2 prs left out from the bud at N become the 2 outer prs of passives; the l.hand pr from P becomes the innermost pr of passives and the other pr becomes the workers. Each pr is twisted once, then the workers work through the 2 inner prs of passives in wh. st.; twist workers once; (wh. st.; twist) through the outer passives; 1–2 extra twists for the workers; pin; (wh. st. and twist) to the outer passive; wh. st. through 2 prs passives to the first inner hole.

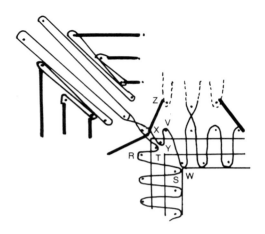

Fig. 1.3 The corner of 'Kirribilli'

The corner

8. This corner should present no problems as it follows the pattern laid down in the main part of the work. Refer to the working diagram, Fig. 1.3; two points only need clarification: the plait from Z to X is linked into the footside *before* the kiss on the corner line is worked, and note the positioning of pin holes before and after the exact corner—on the footside the corner pin has been replaced by two pins, to remove the necessity of using a pin twice, and the 2 extra pins are added, T and Y, one on each side of the kiss. The footside workers will thus travel from W to V to Y, working through 1 pr of passives only; back to X, to the kiss, to T, back to R through one pair of passives and to S.

To complete

9. Work the length desired for the first side and corner; move up and continue similarly for sides 2, 3 and 4. Taking great care to make sure that there are no twists in your work, pin the first 2–3 cm of work back on to the pricking, then join the start to the finish by taking sewings; watch the join very carefully to ensure that the correct pr goes into each starting loop, especially where the prs were hung on 'in pairs' as for the footside passives; here you have 2 separate loops, so one pr will go into each. Knot each pr with a reef knot, and then sew the ends back into the work, taking some to the right of the join and some to the left.

Bennelong

This pattern was named by an interested spectator on a train journey, who asked if I was redesigning the Sydney Opera House—which is situated on the site of the former tram depot on Bennelong Point. The pattern is an example of a simple plaited lace, and introduces picots; as the thread is of medium thickness double picots are used. Single picots used when working in coarse thread will be introduced in Chapter 3. We also use two crossings of plaits, the straightforward windmill crossing and the slightly more complicated six-plait crossing.

Materials: 12 prs of bobbins wound in No. 60 linen lace thread, or the equivalent cotton thread. Thread required on each bobbin should be approximately twice the length of the finished lace, with slightly less for the footside passives.

To work

Following the working diagram, Fig. 1.4, start the footside at Z having 2 prs of workers and 2 prs of passives—make the additional hole at Y to hang these from. Hang the workers in V-formation and the passives in pairs. (As we saw in the last piece of work, you will need a single loop at the end to sew the 2 prs of workers into, and 2 separate loops in which the passives will be sewn.)

1. Hang 2 prs from a supporting pin placed in O—these in succeeding repeats will be used to work the first plait. First, though, work from Z back

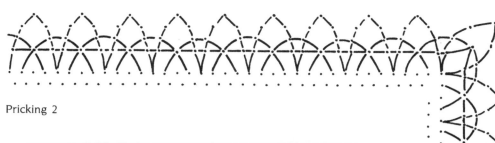

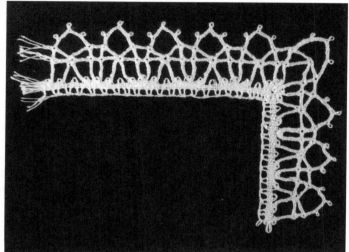

Plate 2 The corner of 'Bennelong'

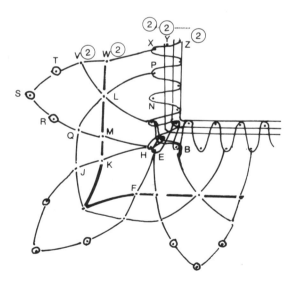

Fig. 1.4 Working diagram for 'Bennelong'

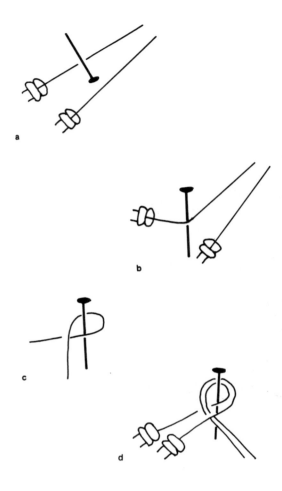

Fig. 1.5 Working a left-hand double picot

and most commonly used crossing of 4 plaits or tallies.

Work the l.h. plait to V where 2 more prs are added in, as at W. Continue the l.h. plait to T where a dot on the pricking (O on the working diagram) indicates a picot; here it is a left-handed picot. Take the l.h. pr from the plait and twist 3–5 times; I prefer the latter so it will largely be used, but you can adapt to your preferences. Following the diagram, Fig. 1.5, place the pin for the hole *over* the outside (l.h.) thread with the point away from you (Fig. 1.5a); twist the pin towards you, then away from you (Fig. 1.5b) and put the pin in the hole (Fig. 1.5c). The second thread of the pair is eased around the pin in the same direction as the first, keeping both threads loose until they are around the pin (Fig. 1.5d). Now allow the two threads to twist together and pull up firmly around the pin. You should feel the click of the threads twisting together, providing that you did not pull the first loop too tightly before adding the second around the pin. You are aiming for a firm twisted loop, and if you find your picots are split when taking out the pins, check that you are working *exactly* as described above, particularly in relation to pulling up. Give 1 twist (r. over l.) to the pr which made the picot; work a wh. st.; twist each pr once (as you are going back into half st.), then continue with the plait. Work l.h. picots at S and R, then plait on to Q. Leave the 2 prs.

2. Now return to the footside and Fig. 1.4. Work to P and out to the footside edge. Take the 2 innermost prs from P (these originally hung from O), and work a plait to L. Here we work a six-plait crossing—see Fig. 1.6. As originally with wh. st., renumber your bobbins for each series of moves, i.e. between moves (a) and (b); (b) and (c), etc.

(a) Cross no. 4 over no. 5; no. 3 under no. 2.
(b) Cross 4 over 3, under 2 and over 1.
(c) Cross 4 over 5, and under 6.
(d) Put up a pin in the centre to hold all steady.
(e) Cross 4 over 5; 3 under 2.
(f) Cross 4 over 3 and under 2.
(g) Cross 4 over 5.

Work each of the three plaits coming from the crossing; the l.h. plait goes to Q where a windmill

to the footside edge through the passives and the 2 prs hanging from O, and complete the changeover stitch. Remove the pin at O and let the 2 prs hang on the workers.

Work the plait from X to W, remembering to keep it just short of the length between the 2 pins. At W add in 2 more prs; hang these from the pin, then, treating each pr of bobbins as if it were a single bobbin, work the first 2 moves of whole stitch: 2 over 3; 2 and 4 over 1 and 3; take out and replace the pin in the centre of the four pairs, then work the final move of wh. st., 2 over 3. These 4 steps—moves 1 and 2 of wh. st.; pin in the centre of the 4 double prs; move 3 of wh. st.— constitute a windmill crossing. This is the simplest

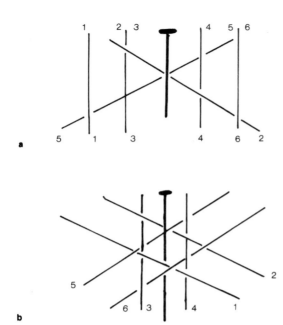

Fig. 1.6 A six-plait (or tallies) crossing: **a.** The first half; **b.** The crossing completed

plait is worked with the two r.h. prs from the crossing to N where it will go back into the footside temporarily.

3. Pick up your workers at whichever point you left them, presumably between P and N—if before N bring in the 2 prs from L at that point, and carry them through the footside until they go out again at B. The prs from the plait from M to H will also be linked into the footside, to come straight out again; such a join is called a V-join. The actual corner follows virtually the same pattern as that of 'Kirribilli': The single hole at the corner is replaced by the two adjacent holes, and there is one extra pin hole on the corner line in the centre of the footside. If needed, turn to Fig. 1.4 and follow the path taken by the workers as shown there.

Work the footside as far as you can go (i.e. to Z), then return to the plaits; the direction taken to work these should be quite clear from the working diagram.

To complete

4. Work each side and corner in turn until they are the desired length. Take sewings, and finally sew the ends back into the work; in plaited lace it is better to omit the reef knot if you are in the habit of using one, as it adds considerably to the bulk in the join in this particular type of lace.

crossing is worked with the pr from R; the centre plait will go to M where a windmill crossing is worked with the prs of a plait from Q; the third

Floral Dance

This insertion can be used to trim an article in conjunction with the edging 'Kirribilli' or it can, of course, be used on its own. Transferred to a smaller graph paper, and worked in a finer thread (e.g. 2 mm graph paper, and worked in 100–120 linen lace thread) they are ideal for trimming a baby's (or doll's) dress. The technique to be introduced is an alternative method of working a V-join, as mentioned in the pattern 'Bennelong', where plaits link directly in and out with the footside.

Materials: 14 prs of bobbins wound in No. 60 linen lace thread or the equivalent cotton or silk thread.

Preparation: No detailed working diagram is given for this insertion as we will use it as a very simple exercise in deciding how many prs to hang on, and where. When you have worked out the number of pairs needed you might like to add them to the basic diagram, given in Fig. 1.7.

We will start on the footsides—being an insertion, of course, there are two! Where will pins

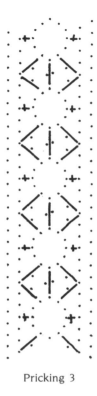

Pricking 3

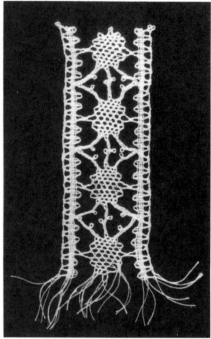

Plate 3 'Floral Dance'

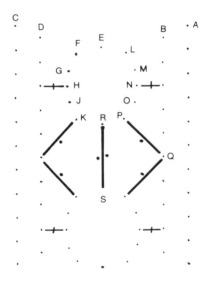

Fig. 1.7 Working diagram for 'Floral Dance'

be hung, and how many? How will they be hung—in V-formation, or in pairs? What will be the role that each pair will play? If in doubt about any of these terms or the roles of the threads, look back to the previous patterns.

Now look at the bud; here there is no indication on the first bud where plaits will come into it, so look down at bud 2 or 3 to help. Each bud is exactly the same, so you will be able to see where you will need pairs coming into each bud, and where pairs will go out from each one. Now, how many pairs will hang from which pin holes for the first bud? Note that in this pattern the kiss is marked in, but quite often it, too, needs to be marked.

Having determined the number of pairs to be hung at each pin hole, one final preparatory move needs to be made; take a pencil, and starting at

E draw in the route your workers will take for the bud; sometimes one must go *either* to the right or to the left to end up at the correct pin hole, sometimes it is immaterial which way you go.

To Work

You should have no problems, providing that you have worked the two previous pieces of lace and are now familiar with the techniques used in them. The following three points, however, need description.

The half stitch bud with a half stitch edging

1. In 'Kirribilli' we worked a (wh. st.; twist) before and after each pin of the half stitch bud. Here I suggest that you use the alternative of just one extra twist to go around the pin, the entire bud being worked in half stitch. You can then compare the two buds, and determine which you prefer.

I must add that I use both versions in appropriate places, and as we come to them, I will say why!

The V-join—alternative method of working

2. In 'Bennelong' we used the straightforward method of working a V-join; the 2 prs from the plait were added to the footside and then taken straight out again. The alternative method reduces bulk at the join, but is not quite so strong. Again, the choice is yours.

Work the footsides, bud and kiss on each side. Work the plait from P to Q (Fig. 1.7). Using the footside workers work through the 2 plait pairs; twist the workers; work back through 1 pair from the plait only. Take the next pair (originally no. 2 from the plait), as workers, and continue the footside, working as far as you can. The two 'non-footside' pairs left at Q become the plait pairs.

Picots on both sides of a plait

3. Dots on either side of a plait indicate a picot on each side. These can be clearly seen marked by the dark line, R to S, on Fig. 1.7, indicating a plait. In modern patterns one dot is usually marginally above the other, and this picot is worked first. In old patterns the dots tend to be all over the place, so you will just have to rely on your own judgement.

In this pattern the higher dot indicates a right-hand picot; this is worked exactly as a left-hand picot except that the pin is placed *under* the *right-hand* thread, with the point facing towards you. The pin is, as before, twisted over and away from you. The second thread follows the first around the pin in the same direction as the first, remembering to keep it all very loose at this stage; the picot is then carefully pulled up, allowing the two threads to twist together (feel the click!), and completed by giving one twist to the pair of threads, right over left. Where picots are being worked on both sides of a plait, the upper one is worked first up to (but including), the twist; then work a wh. st. to keep all 4 threads firmly together, and to hold the picot in place. Twist—as you are going back into half st.—work the second picot, here the l.h. picot; twist the picot threads once, r. over l., then continue with the plait.

Notes

1. How did you hang on your pairs for the insertion? There should have been 2 prs from pins A and C, and 2 prs either from pins B and D or, far preferable, an additional pin hole should have been made between A and B, and between C and D, and the 2 prs. hung from these rather than from B and D. Two further prs. are required at pins E, F and L; none from G and M.

2. Having worked the insertion and the alternative method of working a V-join, you might like to use up some scraps of thread in working a sample of 'Bennelong', using the alternative method of working a V-join, then you can make a direct comparison between the two.

3. As you take each piece of lace off your pillow check the picots. Are they splitting? If so, re-read the instructions for working the picots and follow them *exactly*. The chances are that you are pulling too tightly before passing the second thread around the pin, thus denying them the opportunity to twist together.

2 Tallies—or plaits

Each of the three laces which we are looking at in this book features its own special brand of tallies—and again, just to be difficult, traditional Bedfordshire workers call a tally a '(woven) plait', so don't be alarmed if you are using an old book and find it thus named.

Traditionally the Bedfordshire 'plaits' have square ends, the Cluny tallies are petal-shaped, and the Maltese tallies are fat and squat. Sadly, these traditions are in danger of being merged into one petal-shaped tally, but in this book we will endeavour to keep the old traditions alive!

Preparation: If you have never made a tally before, practice is a good idea. Pin 2 prs of bobbins, wound in any medium to thick thread, on to your pillow. Number them from left to right, 1–2–3–4; *take bobbin no. 2 and, holding it firmly, weave it over no. 3, under no. 4, around and over no. 4, under no. 3, over no. 1 and around and under no. 1. You are now back to the starting place; keep a careful hold of the weaver (no. 2) and carefully ease the first round up into place, keeping nos. 1 and 4 positioned so that the tally is the shape you desire. A petal-shaped tally will have the first round pulled really tightly, while a square-ended tally will need the outer threads positioned so that the end of the tally fills the

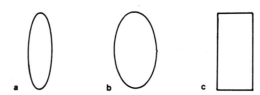

Fig. 2.1 Traditional tally shapes: **a.** petal; **b.** Maltese; **c.** Bedfordshire

space intended for it.** You can try easing up by separating each bobbin between the fingers and easing the worker thread, held between thumb and forefinger of the left hand, up into place; this is probably the best method for working a petal-shaped tally; a square-ended tally can have the threads spaced so that a right angle is formed between nos. 1 and 4; these are held firmly in position by the hands while the weaver is eased into position. The golden rule, however, no matter what shaped tally you are aiming for, is that the weaver must be supported at all times—*never* let it drop as this will immediately ruin the shape of the tally.

Repeat from * to ** as often as needed to barely fill the space, making sure that you keep the tally the intended shape (see later patterns in this chapter).

Daisy Chain

This is a simple insertion which gives plenty of practice in working petal-shaped tallies. Do a good length of it so that you don't have to worry about your tallies in future pieces of lace. Even if you have worked a good number of square torchon-style tallies you are strongly advised to work at least a practice piece of this lace.

Materials: 14 prs of bobbins wound in DMC No. 70 Fils à Dentelles (tatting cotton) or the new size of this thread, No. 80; or No. 60–80 linen lace thread. Decide for yourself how you want your lace to look, bearing in mind that your tension may vary considerably, one way or the other, from mine.

To Work

Apart from the tallies there are no new techniques in Daisy Chain. We will use a twisted footside as it provides a better contrast with the solid-looking tallies. *Following the working diagram, Fig. 2.2, hang 2 prs of bobbins at A in V-formation, and 2 prs at B in pairs. The twisted footside is worked: changeover stitch at A; (wh. st.; twist each pr once, r. over l.) with each of the footside passives; 1–2 extra twists to the workers; pin; (wh. st.; twist twice); 1–2 extra twists; pin in D; changeover stitch.

Continue with the footside, adding in 2 prs at C to work the tally. It is not a good idea to get

Pricking 4

Plate 4 'Daisy Chain'

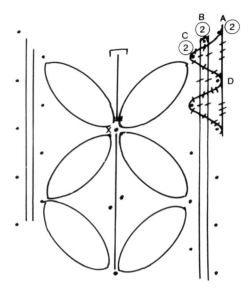

Fig. 2.2 Working diagram for 'Daisy Chain' pattern. N.B. Plait between [and] is only relevant for repeats, not at the start

too far ahead in any one part of the pattern, e.g. the footside, as the pins used sometimes prohibit freedom of movement in pulling up tallies, etc., so you probably will not work more than 1–2 further pins at this stage.

Work a petal-shaped tally from C to X; if desired put a temporary supporting pin on the centre of the tally at X**.

Repeat from * to ** on the l.h. side, reversing each part. When working the tally the first round of weaving will be pulled up so that it is really tight; each succeeding round will be slightly longer, so that you are getting a petal which is a true petal shape; it should reach its greatest width in the centre. Having reached this point, start to decrease the width *very gradually* so that your final round, just short of the pin, is pulled right up again—see Fig. 2.1 for the shape you are aiming for!

Remove the supporting pin; as the tallies should have finished at a point they will not pull out of shape, nor will they come undone! Add in 2 extra prs on X (in V-formation) and work a 6-plait crossing (see p.16 if in doubt). The r.h. and l.h. 2 prs are each used to work a tally, while the 2 centre prs work a plait with a picot on each side halfway down (see p.19).

Where the tallies form a V-join with the footside, you can use either the method described on p.17, or the alternative method (p.19) of linking a plait with the footside.

Repeat the pattern as often as required, and finish off, either by joining the insertion while on the pillow, or by knotting and cutting off, and disposing of the ends in a manner appropriate to the end use of the lace.

Helianthus

This pattern is based on a motif frequently found in Maltese lace. It introduces the fatter, squat tallies which are mostly used in this form of bobbin lace. I have a much-travelled pair of silk Maltese handkerchiefs, one of which is identical to that photographed in Thomas Wright's *The Romance of the Lace Pillow.* Mine was purchased in Malta, being then taken to New Zealand at the end of World War I. From there they resided in the UK for about twenty years before returning to the Antipodes, but this time to Australia. These edgings both feature the sunflower motif—the large round centre surrounded by 16 short squat tallies.

I have used this motif as part of a decorative strip, which is started and finished with a complete circle; if preferred, the pattern can be used as a continuous braid to trim an article such as a lampshade. It also lends itself to the use of colour. On the baby's dress in Colour Plate 1, the pattern is worked in a fine white thread. The start and finish will be marginally different if you

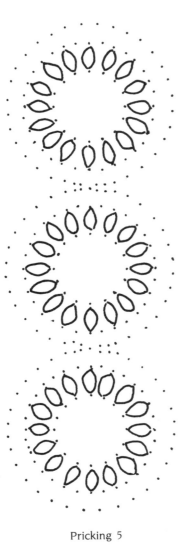

Pricking 5

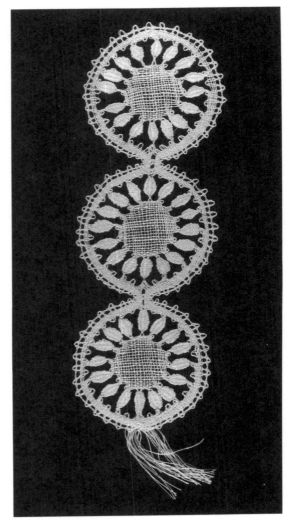

Plate 5 'Helianthus'

choose the decorative strip or the continuous lace edging, so we will look at the strip first.

Materials: 24 prs of bobbins wound in No. 80 linen lace thread or its equivalent. For a strip of three pattern repeats you will need to put at least 1.5 m on each bobbin.

To Work
Referring to Fig. 2.3 and the working diagram, Fig. 2.4, hang 2 prs on a pin in A—these are the workers. Lay the passives for the outer ring across the pillow, holding them temporarily in place by pins placed at B and C. You will need a minimum of 6 individual bobbins each side (3 prs of passives), but as you will have a slightly denser trail than this at the end of the strip I would suggest that you lay in 10–14 prs of bobbins, making 5–7 pairs each side so that the start and finish appear almost identical. The remainder of the prs will be added in as they are needed to work the tallies.

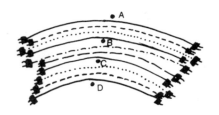

Fig. 2.3 Hanging the bobbins for a double-sided start

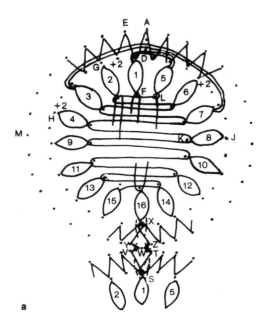

a

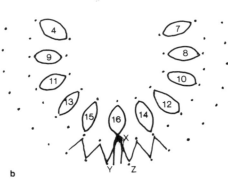

b

Fig. 2.4 Working diagrams for 'Helianthus' pattern: **a.** the start of the decorative strip; **b.** the finish of the decorative strip

1. Using the l.h. pr at A as workers and *having a trail with a twisted edge, start the trail, working across to the right to D where the first 2 prs are taken out, to work tally 1.

First, though, take the workers out to the outer edge putting up a pin in E; work the tally from D to F, making it considerably fatter in the centre than for normal petal tallies—see Fig. 2.1 for comparisons.** This is not as easy as it sounds, as you will see from my sample. You will probably have to work hard to keep the tallies the correct shape; think about coming in before you actually do—i.e. in a tally consisting of 16 woven rounds, start to think about decreasing the width after round 7. This helps to avoid a sudden decrease in width, leading to unevenness on the edges of the tallies. When you are satisfied (or nearly so!) with your tally, put up a supporting pin if desired.

Return to the trail and continue to work as from * to **. You do not have sufficient pairs in the trail to leave them out to work all the tallies, so it will be necessary to add in 2 prs at each of the pins G and H to work the tallies starting at these pins; then you should have sufficient pairs left in the trail to leave out prs to work tallies 1 and 3. When the edge pin at M has been placed, leave the left side and return to A where the second pair is taken as workers for the r.h. side of the trail. This is worked identically to the first side, the last tally to be worked being No. 8, from J to K.

The flower centre

2. Here again we have a slight deviation from what may be thought of as the 'normal' method of working. Have a close look at the working diagram, Fig. 2.4a: to keep a good shape, and to avoid overcrowding, you will notice that the start for working the bud is pin L. A pin is placed in F between the 2 prs coming from tally no. 1, and they immediately become passives. The r.h. pr from tally 5 become your workers, weaving in wh. st. through the l.h. pr from tally 5, the 2 prs from tally 1 and the 2 prs from tally 2. Twist and pin as usual.

Work the whole bud, bringing in the 2 prs from each of the tallies 1–8, and then leaving out the

2 prs for tallies 9–16, working the last 6 prs as at the start.

3. Work each of the tallies 9–16, placing a temporary pin in the lower pin hole if desired. You will find it necessary to push these right down.

The r.h. trail

4. Now return to the r.h. trail. Continue working it, bringing in 2 prs from each of the tallies as you reach them. When you have a build up of prs, giving you 6–7 prs, you can start to *throw out* prs. This is done by taking one of the prs which have been in the trail for the longest distance and just laying it to the back of the work. *Never* take an edge pr—in this case the twisted edge pr—or the first pr after (or before) the twisted edge. The best pr to take is the next one—as it is lying now, no. 3 from the outer edge. These prs are being thrown out because the trail is too dense, but *do* make sure that the work is sufficiently dense to support cut ends at a later stage, particularly if you are working in a mercerised cotton. You will probably need to throw out a pair on each of two successive rows—only throw out more than a single pair on a row if it is absolutely necessary.

Continue the trail, bringing in prs from the tallies and leaving out where appropriate until you have placed the pin in Z. Leave this side of the trail, return to X and complete the second side similarly up to Y (refer to Fig. 2.4b).

Bring the workers in turn through the remaining prs of passives to X; bring in one pr on each side from tally no. 16, link the 2 prs of workers with (wh. st.; twist; pin in X)#. For the remainder of the narrow 'bridge' between the two adjoining motifs, the two sides have to be worked together; *take the l.h. pr. of workers from X and work wh. st. through the l.h. pr from tally 16, and all those you have left on the l.h. side to Y. Pin**.

Repeat from * on the r.h. side using pin Z. Now work each of the sides to W (the central pin) and link the workers with (wh. st.; etc.). Work the sides in turn to V and T, then to S where the workers link for a final time; this completes the bridge and the workers in turn continue with their respective sides of the second circle. Note that the first pins appear to be at a strange angle from the link pin S; do not leave these pins out.

To complete the decorative strip

5. Work until you reach the point # as described in section 4. Take the two workers out to the outside edge—no pin. Take one bobbin from each side and, starting in the centre, knot each pair of bobbins with a reef knot, ensuring that the passives are taut before they are knotted. It is advisable to leave all the bobbins on until you have checked that your knots are correct, and that each thread is knotted with its opposite partner; then, having tied your last knots with the workers on each side, cut off the bobbins leaving a piece of thread from each approximately 10 cm long. These ends will either be sewn back into the work, taking one from each pair away from the central knot, or they can be taken back through the mounting fabric if used, and then either knotted off or sewn in, depending on the end use of the lace. Carefully trim all ends left in the work where bobbins have been thrown out.

For a continuous strip you may prefer to start at the join between two circles, i.e. at W in Fig. 2.4a. Before starting to work you will need to extend the pattern so that you do not spend too much time in moving up. This can be achieved by pricking the first 2–3 pattern repeats, inserting one or more sheet(s) of moderately thin paper such as bank typing paper between the pattern and the pricking card; prick through all layers, then carefully remove the paper pricking which you now have, and match it (or them) up with the original pattern to give you the desired length. Alternatively, you can use a photocopier, but remember that the resulting copies are inevitably slightly distorted, and adjustments will most likely have to be made.

Note: If you run out of thread on a bobbin it is easy to join in a new thread in the centre of a tally. Hang your new thread from a pin at the back of your work, and let it double with one of the passives of the tally, i.e. you weave around two threads together instead of a single thread, work the stitch at the end of the tally, then unwind the pair of threads from the bobbin, put the 'old' thread to the back of your work, and continue with the single 'new' thread. Another good place to join in threads is in a plait; here you similarly work with two threads together for the length of the plait and for the stitch at the end of it, making sure to treat the plait firmly so that the additional thread causes the plait to alter in appearance as little as possible.

Lulu

This motif introduces the typical square-ended tally of Bedfordshire, which can also be seen in the pattern 'Lizzie', starting on page 79. It can be worked in one colour, as in Plate 6 or in two or three colours, as in Colour Plate 5.

Materials: 20 prs of bobbins, wound in No. 70–80 linen lace thread, or the equivalent cotton or silk thread. The white motif was worked in No. 80 linen lace thread, and the coloured motif in DMC Fils à Dentelles (No. 70–80), in two shades of pink, and white. You will need 5 prs with approximately 1 m on each bobbin for the outer edge workers and for the two outer tallies; 3 prs with approximately 40 cm on each bobbin for the outer edge passives, and the rest with approximately 60 cm on each bobbin.

To Work

Following the working diagram, Fig. 2.5, hang on bobbins as indicated both in the diagram and above. The passives for the edge circle should be hung in pairs and the rest in V-formation.

1. *Start the outer ring, adding in 2 prs for the first spoke at B, and a further pr at C for the tally. In theory you can continue the ring until you reach D, but this is not advisable as the pins tend to get in the way when working the tallies, particularly when easing them up into place. Therefore, work to approximately E and then leave the circle and return to the first spoke. Work the plait (leg) to F; then work a windmill crossing with the three pairs—you use *two prs* and the two single bobbins to work the crossing, so it will be (a pr as no. 2, which crosses and a single thread, no. 3; 2 single threads crossing the 2 prs; and finally a pair crossing a single thread). This leaves the two single threads to the left and the

2 prs to the right. Don't worry that the pairs have changed places—in fact this can be a definite advantage if you are running short of thread on a bobbin.

2. Now return to the upper tally. Where you have a single pr coming from 2 adjoining pin holes it invariably indicates a square-ended tally, and care must be taken to ensure that such a tally is a clear oblong shape, trying to avoid any lumps and bumps. The actual weaving is, of course, identical to that for the petal-shaped tally. To keep the shape at the end, after working the final round of weaving immediately put up pins in the base holes to support the work, i.e. K and L in the first tally. Carefully leave this tally and work the first lower tally with the prs added in at G and H. Pin and leave.

3. Continue the outer ring to somewhere between O and D, adding in 2 more prs at O, then start the second spoke. Great care will be needed when joining in the prs from the tallies to the plait at K, M, N and just below L. At these points you have 3 prs only, so again the windmill crossing is worked with 2 × 2 threads, and 2 × 1 thread, as described above. As the square end of the upper tallies does not quite reach the spoke, 1–2 extra twists will be needed to make a neat join. Many readers will know that there are two alternative methods of finishing a tally when it is worked, as described in the introduction to this chapter. The weaver can be left in its starting position, i.e. no. 2, or it can be carried on one place and become no. 3 with the original no. 3 becoming no. 2. As it is normally easier to achieve a good shape when finishing off the side which does *not* contain the weaver first, it is best to carry the weaver on one place in the first half of the

Pricking 6

Plate 6 'Lulu'

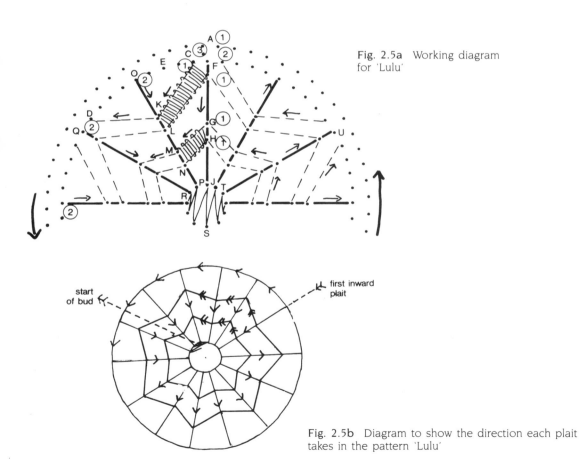

Fig. 2.5a Working diagram for 'Lulu'

Fig. 2.5b Diagram to show the direction each plait takes in the pattern 'Lulu'

pattern, i.e. when taking the spokes in to the centre, and reversing it in the second half, i.e. when taking the spokes out from the centre, leave the weaver in second place at the end of the tally.

4. Work the second spoke to P.**

5. Repeat from * to ** (i.e. twice more), substituting 'join in' for 'add in' pairs where appropriate. You now have 6 prs in the centre ready to work a small half stitch bud. A bud used as here, both for decoration and to cross a large group of threads, is always started from the centre of the group of threads, here at pin R (Fig. 2.5). Normally it will be necessary to trace the route of the workers to determine the exact starting point (for you can sometimes have a choice!), the initial direction, and the correct finishing point. This can be done either on your paper pattern with a pencil, or using a pin on your pricking.

6. In the sample (Plate 6) the bud was worked with

(half st.; one extra twist to the workers; pin; half st.) at each end of the row, but you can choose between the two methods—see pages 13 and 18 if necessary. Complete the bud.

7. We are now ready to start working the spokes outwards and the remainder of the tallies. The first spoke will start at S and will be identical to the spoke radiating from T to U. Do not forget what I said a few paragraphs back about finishing off a tally! No further instructions should be needed, so you can now complete the motif.

Finishing off
Finish off by taking sewings into the starting holes, and knotting off each pair in turn. As this is a decorative motif you will almost certainly be able to take your ends to the back of the mounting fabric and knot them off there to avoid the bulk in the join which tends to occur when sewing the ends back into a small piece of lace.

3 Headsides and footsides

In the introduction I said that the ability to work a basic footside and one in which the workers and passives are twisted between each stitch—commonly called a 'twisted footside'—is assumed. These are the two footsides we have used so far. Two further footsides are commonly used in this group of laces, the kat-stitch foot and the cucumber foot, together with an infrequently used variation of the kat-stitch foot. These we will explore in this chapter, together with three of the

headings which are most commonly used, the nine-pin head; the heading commonly called the Cluny head and the simple curved heading. These footsides and headings are combined to make three simple patterns.

First, though, we will look at the basic *nine-pin heading*. This pattern is so named because one pattern repeat consists of nine pins being placed, as in Fig. 3.1.

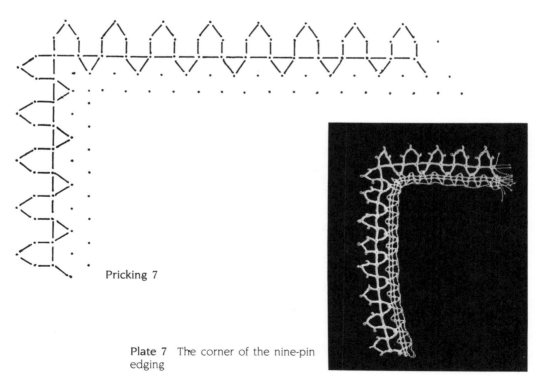

Pricking 7

Plate 7 The corner of the nine-pin edging

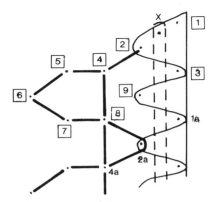

Fig. 3.1 The nine-pin edging

Materials: 8 prs of bobbins wound in No. 70 DMC Cordonnet as in the sample shown in Plate 7 or, for a slightly firmer lace, DMC Cordonnet No. 60 or linen lace thread No. 60.

To Work

Following the working diagram, Fig. 3.1, hang 2 prs from (1) in V-formation, 2 prs from an additional pin placed in X (hung in pairs), 2 prs from (2) and 2 prs from (4), both in V-formation.

1. Work a twisted footside to 2 where 2 additional pairs are added in to work the first plait. As before, in the 'Bennelong' pattern, Chapter 1, work the footside back to (3) before working the plait. Watch the length of your plait closely—you should have no problems with either the mechanism of plaiting or of tension by now, but constant care is needed, no matter how experienced you are, to prevent the plaits being either too long or too short; probably too many suffer from being too long, so follow the advice of one of my students and work the plait the length you think it should be, then undo one stitch; we call this 'Pat's rule' after her. I now use this method and it is pretty foolproof!

2. Add in a further 2 prs (already hanging around the pin) in V-formation at (4); work a windmill crossing, taking out and replacing the pin after move 2 (see p.16) if necessary; then completing the stitch. Work a plait to (8), putting a temporary pin between the 2 prs at (8) if desired.

3. Now work around the V. Plait to (5); double picot; plait to (7); double picot; plait to (8). Cross the 2 plaits at (8) with a windmill crossing; plait the straight one to 4a, then the diagonal plait to 2a.

4. Return to the footside where the workers were left at (3). (9) is a snatch pin (with no plait or tally coming into it or out of it); 1a is a normal changeover stitch. The V-link of the plaits with the footside can be worked in either method, as on pp. 17 and 19.

The corner

5. The corner is quite straightforward; the exact corner pin is used twice and the second time it is best treated as a snatch pin to reduce bulk at the corner. You are working on the wrong side of the finished lace, and when the edging is attached to the mounting fabric the little loop is just caught into place with the straight footside edge.

Work the desired length on each side and the required number of corners, then finish off by taking sewings, knotting and sewing the ends back in.

This simple, quick to execute edging makes an ideal trim for a small article such as a lavender or pot-pourri bag (sachet), for a handkerchief edging, or for a trim around a collar, neckline or sleeves, but it does need care in ironing if used for an article which needs frequent laundering.

Marguerite

This pattern was drawn from an old Bedfordshire pricking which I 'inherited' with a box of old

wooden bobbins around 1960—in the days when antique bobbins were still freely available. On the

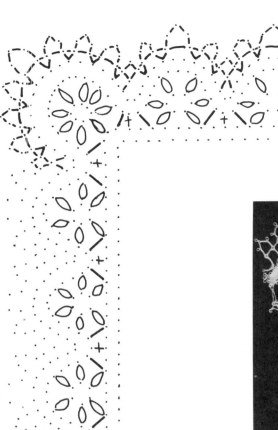

Pricking 8

Plate 8a 'Marguerite', worked in No. 30
DMC Retors d'Alsace thread

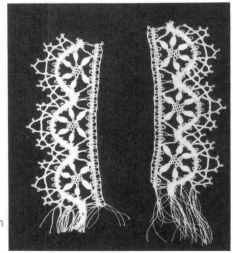

Plate 8b 'Marguerite', worked in No. 80 linen
lace thread on the left, and No. 100 linen
lace thread on the right.

original pattern the tallies were clearly marked as petals. The corner has been simplified, and the whole pattern trued up. As can be seen from the worked samples in Plate 8 it, in common with many Bedfordshire and Cluny patterns, is reasonably tolerant where thread sizes are concerned, and you can choose the size you prefer and that most suitable for the end use, and/or the mounting fabric for your lace. You should, too, by now be beginning to have a feel for your own work—is your natural tension in this work tight or loose? This of course will also influence your choice of thread to pricking.

Materials: 18–20 prs of bobbins wound in the thread of your choice using the illustrations in Plate 8 as a guide. The sample with a corner was worked in No. 30 retors d'Alsace, and used 20 prs of bobbins. In addition you will need four extra pairs for the corner.

To Work

One of the more difficult aspects of these laces is the start, where you have to determine both where you will start and how many pairs to put on and where. We have already looked at this in a simple way in 'Floral Dance' in Chapter 1. This pattern is slightly more complicated but the same principles apply. The best place to start a trail is usually at the base of a curve as the majority of pairs will be in the trail at this point, and pairs usually leave the trail after this to work a different part of the pattern; true, it is much easier to start at the top of a curve where you have a more clearly defined number of pairs but this produces a less satisfactory result, and where the lace is being joined at the finish, the join is much more apparent. It is the number of pairs to put in the trail at the start which causes the problems, so we will work this one through. Always aim to have the exact number of pairs in the start that you will need; plus or minus 1–2 pairs is acceptable, but no more, otherwise the base of the trail at the start will look decidedly thinner than that in future pattern repeats. Also, remember that you do not necessarily start at the first pin hole on your pricking—*you* choose where to start, and it may well be that your choice is several pattern repeats from the start, or it may be that just a

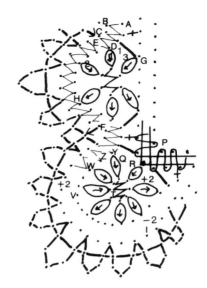

Fig. 3.2   Working diagram for 'Marguerite' pattern

few pin holes are omitted . . . don't worry, these will be used in any following repeats! My preference is not to start where there is a kiss, so I would choose either rows A–B or C–D in Fig. 3.2. Let us choose A–B, as it is slightly harder!

1. Start the process of working out the numbers of pairs required by assessing the number of passives which you will need for the trail; I call these basic trail bobbins 'constant pairs' as they are in the trail all the time, together with one pair of workers. In addition to these constant pairs you will need to start the trail with an extra number of pairs which will leave the trail at given points to work the tallies and plaits which leave the trail; as I have already said, it is much easier to add these pairs in as you reach the points where they are needed, but this method does make the first part of your lace thinner than subsequent repeats, so it is worth taking the extra trouble to work out the number of additional pairs you need to put in the trail at the start so that you have sufficient to leave out from the trail in order to work these first few plaits and tallies. In this pattern you will need to put in an additional 6 prs at the start; 4 prs for the first 2 flower petals, and 2 prs for the plait from D to G. Remember that the kiss is made with the workers, so no prs actually go out or in here.

2. Now turn your attention to the left-hand side of the trail (as you work); how many come in or go out here?—yes, 2 come in at E, and all the rest come in and go straight out again, so we only need to worry about the 2 prs coming in. Now we must see if we can compensate for any of these prs by counting in some which will go out later; as in 'Floral Dance' this is best done by looking down a pattern repeat. Two prs will come in at A to go out again at D, which we have counted as needing 2 prs, so these can be subtracted from the grand total so far arrived at. This leaves us with 4 prs needed at present, in addition, of course, to the constant prs. Now repeat with the l.h. side of the trail; are there any prs coming in near the start which will not be needed right now? Yes, those from E we have already seen do not go out to work a plait until pin F on the trail, so in between the points E and F they can be used to work one of the tallies, say No. 2, and they will be back in the trail at H, several pin holes before you reach F where they go out to work a plait.

3. So, we now have the final total—I used 5 prs of constant passives when working in No. 100 linen lace thread, so we have 5 prs + 1 pr (the workers) + 4 prs needed to leave the trail almost immediately to work a couple of tallies for which we have no compensating prs coming in to the trail; a total of 10 prs to be hung from the pin holes along line A–B; you will need to make a couple of extra holes between these 2 points so that the bobbins are hung in a regular manner (as when working a footside). Remember that those bobbins which will become workers are best hung on in V-formation, while those which will become passives are best hung on in pairs so that they have separate loops for the final join.

4. Having already worked the 9-pin edging, and remembering all that we have learnt so far, you should have no problems in working the basic pattern until you reach the corner.

The corner

5. Refer again to the working diagram, Fig. 3.2. Work the footside to P and the trail to V. Continue the trail, leaving out 2 prs for tallies at each of the pins Z and W, and adding in 2 prs at V (to work the tally V to T). You can now continue the trail for a further few pins, then leave.

Return to the footside; if not already worked, make the plait from Y to Q; work the footside to Q then back towards the edge through 2 prs and leave the workers to become passives. Take the passives nearest to the main body of work as new workers; work through the 2 prs of the plait, through the remaining pr of original passives and leave—to become the second pr of footside passives. Finally, take the last pr of original passives—those nearest to the straight edge—to become a new pr of workers.

As you will have added in 2 additional prs at V, these will need to be thrown out when the trails are of sufficient density to hold the eventual cut ends. Here I would throw out *one thread* at a time, as there are only the 2 to go out.

This method of working a corner, with slight variations to accommodate different numbers of passives, etc. gives an uncluttered look to the corner, and is very often used when working corners in laces of this group.

Glifada

This pattern introduces the heading which is known as the 'scalloped head' or 'Cluny heading'. The footside used is the kat foot, named because in appearance it has similarities to the kat-stitch ground found in point ground lace which in turn was named, as are several aspects of East Midlands lace, for Queen Katherine of Aragon who, after her banishment by King Henry VIII, settled in the Bedfordshire village of Ampthill, and is reputed to have taught the villagers the

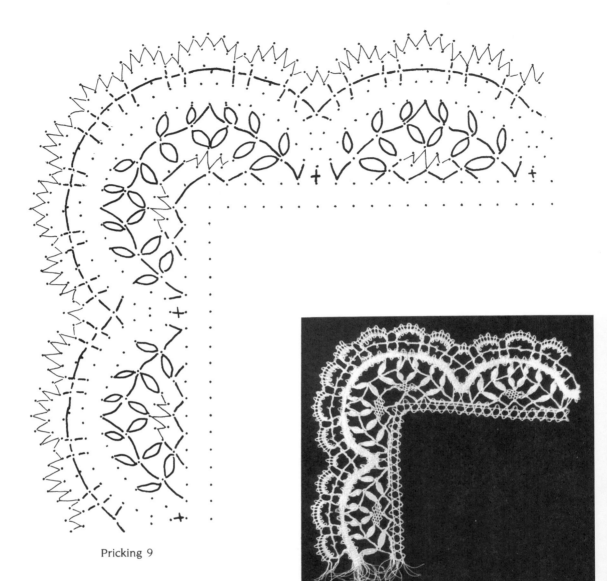

Pricking 9

Plate 9 The corner of 'Glifada'

lacemaking which she learned in her native Spain. The trail, 'garlands' of leaves, and diamonds should present no problems if you have worked the earlier patterns in the book.

Materials: 23–24 prs of bobbins wound in No. 60 linen lace thread (as in the sample), or equivalent.

Preparation: Before starting this pattern, work a short length of the footside for practice, using the working diagram, Fig. 3.3, as a guide. 4 prs are needed for the basic footside, plus any additional prs which will come into—and thus go out of!—the footside at any given place.

Hang 2 prs at Pin A and 2 prs at pin B. *Work

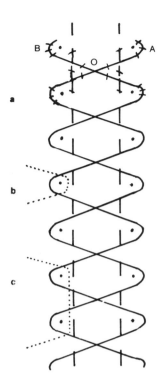

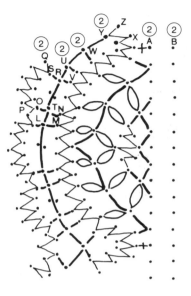

Fig. 3.3 The kat-stitch footside: **a** the plain footside; **b** joining a plait with a V-join; **c** joining a plait with a U-join

Fig. 3.4 Working diagram for 'Glifada'

(wh. st. and twist each pr. once, with 1–2 extra twists to go around the pin) **with the 2 prs at A. Repeat from * to ** with the 2 prs at B.

Take the 2 centre prs and work (wh. st. and twist) with them, *** thus changing over the position of the 'workers'.

Repeat from * to *** as and where needed.

Where prs come into the footside to link the two parts of the work, or to be carried on to another part of the pattern, they are best left untwisted; if twisted they take up too much space and detract from the overall appearance. In Fig. 3.3c work (wh. st.; twist each pr once) with the passives and the pr coming from the centre (your workers); 2 wh. sts. with the prs coming in from the plait; twist 2–3 times for the pin, then complete either method of working the V-join, as preferred or as indicated.

Where prs are added in to be carried in the footside they are worked in plain wh. st. inside the passives, with the twist from the (wh. st. and twist) clearly visible.

To Work

Following the working diagram, Fig. 3.4, hang prs as indicated. The number of pairs needed for the trail are worked out as in the pattern 'Marguerite' which you have just worked. Don't forget that *you* choose the starting point; mine looks rather strange in the sample, Plate 9, but I am assuming that the lace will be joined into a square or rectangle and I find that an arrangement like this gives the neatest join. Do look at future pattern repeats to see what will happen to pins W and U!

A. The trail

Start with the trail at Z. At X a kiss will join the trail to the footside, so start the footside, working the kiss on the 1st inner pin. You will then need to work a little more of the trail to have the prs needed for the first plait which links with the trail at W.

Continue the footside, trail plaits and tallies to V, using Plate 9 as a guide to the positioning of plaits, and noting that 2 prs are added in (with a windmill crossing) at pins S and T.

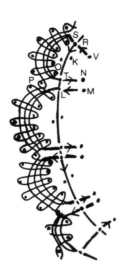

Fig. 3.5 The scalloped (Cluny) head

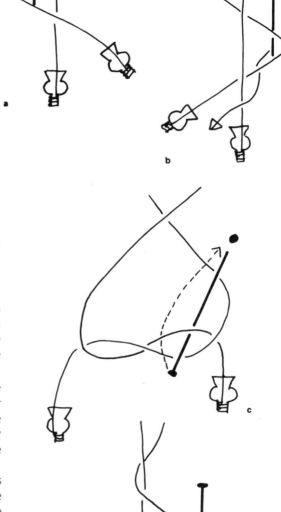

Work (wh. st.; twist; pin; wh. st; twist) with the 2 prs at Q.

B. The Scalloped or Cluny heading
This headside is worked with 6 prs of bobbins, 4 for the scallops and 2 for the plait which runs parallel to the trail. When commencing the head 2 new prs are hung on a pin placed in Q; one becomes the workers for the scallop, and the other the headside passives (see Fig. 3.5).

1. Work a plait from V to R where it links with the plait, which I will call the 'parallel plait' for identification; then work a windmill crossing. The 2 l.h. prs plait to S where they are picked up by the workers from Q, and these 2 prs become the lower passives for the scallop.

   The workers zig-zag to P where the pin is worked, as at Q. The 2 prs which became the lower passives are plaited to T (to await the parallel plait from R).

2. With the 2 remaining prs from R work a plait to the r.h. dot (K) which indicates a picot. As we are using a comparatively thick thread for this type of lace, and the space between the parallel plait and both the scallop and trail is not large, a single picot is most suitable here:

(i) Take the 2 r.h. threads from the plait, and give this pr one twist.

Fig. 3.6 A single picot

36

(ii) Put the pin under the right thread.

(iii) Put the pin (and the thread) over the l.h. thread (Fig. 3.6a).

(iv) Pull the pin to the right, and with the point towards you, over the cross (Fig. 3.6b).

(v) Tip the pin over so that the point goes away from you, under the crossed thread and up between these two threads to the right (Fig. 3.6c).

(vi) Put the pin in the picot hole, and carefully pull all up into place (Fig. 3.6d).

Work (wh. st. and twist) with the 2 plait prs then work a second picot as (i)–(vi) above with the l.h. pr and putting the pin to the left of the plait. Again, work (wh. st.; twist) before continuing with the plait.

3. Complete the plait to the crossing, then work a windmill crossing at T with the 2 prs from O, then plait from T to N and from T to L.

4. The remaining 2 scallops and the mini-scallop linking 2 adjoining pattern repeats are worked as 1, 2 and 3 above.

The corner

5. While looking very large and complicated, the corner is in fact very simple. The only problem it should present is at the actual corner spot on the footside.

Work the footside, garland, diamond, trail and heading up to the actual corner line. Give your pillow a quarter turn so that the footside of the second part of the corner is on the right, and then work the heading, trail, garland and diamonds as far as you can go—the widest part of the half stitch diamond.

Return to the footside, and if not already there, work to pins C and D (Fig. 3.7). Work the centre crossing with the usual prs from C and D; take the pr from D around the corner pin E, and the other pr from the crossing to J as usual; this pr works wh. st. through the passives then 2 twists—note the extra twist—(wh. st.; 2–3 twists) through the inner passives, and use pin E a second time. Leave the 3 prs here.

Take the inner passives as workers; (wh. st.; 2–3 twists through the 2 prs of the plait from F; pin in G; wh. st. through the 2 plait prs); twist workers and leave.

Return to E; regain the inner original workers which were left at A and work (wh. st.; 2 twists)

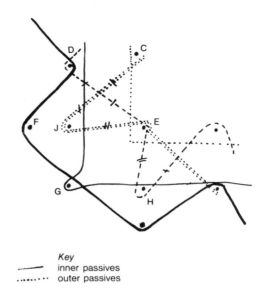

Key
——— inner passives
········· outer passives

Fig. 3.7 The footside portion of the corner

through the outer passives; (wh. st.; twist through the inner passives); pin in H; (wh. st.; twist) through the inner passives.

Regain the second pr of original workers which were left at E; work through the inner passives as usual, and then complete the centre crossing.

To complete

6. Work the required lengths on all four sides, together with three further corners, to complete. Take sewings into the starting loops, then carefully sew the ends back into the work.

Notes

1. The kat-stitch foot: occasionally in old examples of this type of lace the footside is worked with a pin in the centre—in this case pin D in Fig. 3.3 is worked (wh. st.; twist; pin; wh. st.; twist).

2. The heading is sometimes worked without the plait which runs parallel to the trail in this pattern.

3. *Check!* Are your plaits and tallies the perfect length, and with a good firm tension? Remember that there should be no buckling in either, nor should there be gaps before a crossing or join. Work hard to get them perfect.

Venus

In this mat we introduce cucumbers, used both in a cucumber foot and to link parts of a pattern as a substitute for a kiss. The outer trail can be used as a heading, or a curved plait with picots can be added outside the trail, giving a lighter appearance.

Materials: 29 or 31 prs of bobbins, wound in No. 80 linen lace thread, or equivalent cotton thread.

Preparation: One-third of the pricking only is given, so you will need to reproduce the pattern twice more, then piece them together to make the whole pricking.

To Work

The mat is worked as two units; the first extends from the heading to the inside of the two concentric circles—point N on the working diagram; Fig. 3.8 omits the central 9 petals and centre which together make unit 2. Unit 1 is worked first.

1. Starting on the imaginary line from A to N make additional pin holes on the lines A to B and

C to D, then hang a total of 11 prs of bobbins on the line A to B, and 8 prs of bobbins on line C to D. I used 2 prs of passives and 1 pr of workers in each of the concentric footside rings, but you may prefer a third pr of passives, or to put the regular footside (sometimes known as the 'straight edge') on the inside ring; in either of these cases you will, of course, need to adjust the total number of pairs. The remainder of bobbins to be used will be hung as indicated on the working diagram.

Work the first row of the outer trail from A to B; leave.

Work the first row of the inner trail from D to C; put the inner prs aside (for a plait); leave.

2. Take the workers from each of these trails; put up a pin under each pr of workers if you have not already done so. Work a small tally to fill the space between the 2 pins X and Y in Fig. 3.9, but *not* large enough to fill the rectangular space between 4 adjoining pins; the tally in this instance needs to be just large enough to be visible and to do its job of linking the 2 adjoining trails.

The plaited ground

3. We now have all the pairs ready to work the plaited ground. Two pairs are waiting at D and 2 at L; the remaining 4 prs can be added in at P with a windmill crossing, or 2 prs can be added in at each of J and K; the first alternative will

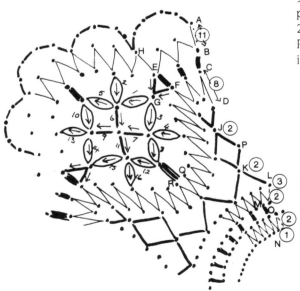

Fig. 3.8 Working diagram for 'Venus'

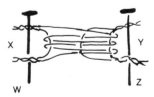

Fig. 3.9 A cucumber showing the 4 individual threads

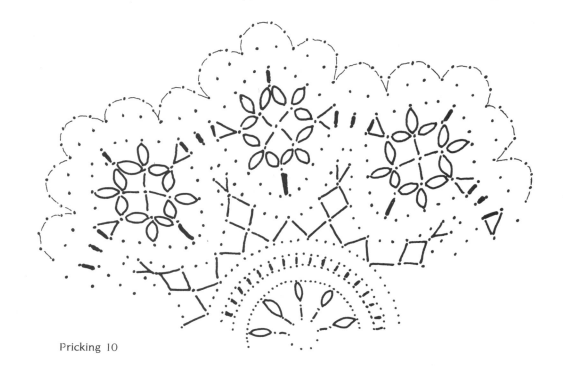

Pricking 10

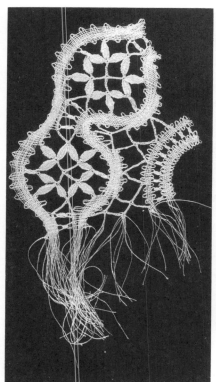

Plate 10b 'Venus', with a looped picot edge

Plate 10a A portion of 'Venus', with a straight edge

39

necessitate an additional sewing at the end of the work, the latter means that you are having to join into 2 plaits. Work the plaits and windmill crossings as far as you can go, returning to the footside rings and the inner trail when necessary. Three plaits (6 pairs) will be added into the trail, the l.h. prs from J firstly, then the r.h. pr from J and the l.h. pr from K.

The group of tallies and plaits

4. This should present no difficulties if you carefully follow the arrows to show the direction of working, and the numerical order of working, both of which are given on the working diagram. The cucumbers linking the tallies with the two trails need slightly more care than those previously worked; in the first place they are rather longer, and secondly the inner pin hole of each tally is also supporting the tally, so I find it best to put up the pin in the hole before working the cucumber, then to take it out and replace it with a wh. st. after the cucumber has been worked. Note that you have a choice of pin holes at Q and R; try both and see which you prefer, then stick to that throughout. The outer cucumber is worked with the trail workers and the l.h. pr from tally 5; the inside cucumber with the workers from the inner trail and the r.h. pr from tally 8. As before, be sure to put supporting pins in the next pin holes below the cucumber for temporary support.

Having completed the tallies and plaits, return to the two trails and work them, and the heading if used, to the end of the first pattern repeat, adding in pairs from the tallies where indicated.

5. Repeat the above 8 times, then take sewings, knot the pairs following each sewing, and sew the ends back into your work if desired. I find it easiest to just knot the pairs—sometimes adding a third half-stitch for extra security—in a mat, as there tends to be a marked ridge if all the ends are sewn in along one line.

The central motif

6. If you look closely at this you will see that there are 9 petals—a fact which does not add to simplicity!

You will probably have enough thread left on at least some of your bobbins to work this—you

Fig. 3.10 The centre of the mat—part 2 in working

will need 10 prs of bobbins, and try to have at least 0.5 m without knots on each bobbin, so knot them together in pairs and wind the knots on to one bobbin of each pr. Sew these in pairs into the appropriate holes in the edge of the inner ring as shown in Fig. 3.10. With each group of 2 prs work a petal-shaped tally to the first pin hole; give each pr a second twist; pin in the centre of the 2 prs then plait to the appropriate hole in the centre circle. When completed you should have 5 plaits ready to be linked in the centre. Take the central pin of the five as your starting point; pin between the 2 prs from the plait if it is not already there, then cover it with a wh. st. Working either to the r. or to the l. to start with, work a wh. st. bud bringing in prs from the plaits at the first 4 pins, and leaving them out at the last 4 pins. This will leave you with 3 groups of 2 prs and the last one will have 4 prs. Work the plaits, using the threads double for the last plait, and gradually throwing out 4 separate threads as the plait and then the tally progresses; you will probably not have them all out before starting the tally, so use some of the supporting threads—not the weaver—double in this final tally.

Sew out the pairs of thread into the appropriate holes, and then knot and either cut off close, or sew the ends back into your work.

Note: If you wish to mount this motif and use it under glass or on a cushion, pillow sham or for some similar purpose, after having taken your final sewings the ends can be taken through your mounting fabric and finished off appropriately. Naturally this reduces bulk considerably.

4 Looking at trails

In bobbin lace of many traditions a continuous winding line called a trail occurs; it is a particular feature of the three laces we are exploring in this book. The trail follows a winding path through the lace, only very occasionally having sharp corners; it can be wide or narrow, a continuous trail or one broken by other features, plain or divided. Each of the three laces we are here concerned with has its own normal use of trails; those we find in Bedfordshire Maltese are nearly always worked in whole stitch; those in Cluny lace are frequently divided, and may be worked in double stitch (wh. st., and twist). While we are looking at three specific features of trails in this chapter, there are many other features which have already been introduced, or which will be used at later stages in this book.

Crossroads

While most lacemakers get the greatest satisfaction from working a pattern which challenges them, there are occasions when a quick, easy pattern is needed for a gift or a presentation; I have used this pattern several times for these purposes.

As the actual crossing used here has no simple name, I am describing it as a 'multi-crossing'.

Materials: 14 prs of bobbins wound in No. 80–90 linen lace thread. It is advisable to fill the bobbins reasonably full to avoid joining in new threads, but of course far less will be needed for the footside passives.

To Work
Hang the bobbins as indicated on the working diagram, Fig. 4.1. When you are quite familiar with the technique of crossing trails you may choose to start at the actual crossing, but for the present we will start just after the crossing. Start with the footside—a twisted one with 2 prs of passives to provide greater contrast with the wh. st. trails. Note that on the inside 2 prs are immediately left out to work the plait from N to O. Continue the footside to Q.

Now turn to the trails. Working both trails in wh. st., start on the outer trail and work from M to P where 2 prs are left out for the plait. Continue to R then leave this trail.

Work the inner trail to S, linking in the 2 prs from the plait from N to O and leaving out 2 prs for the filling—2 plaits, one from P to X and one from S to X, these being crossed in the centre with a windmill crossing. Complete the plaits from X to T and from X to V.

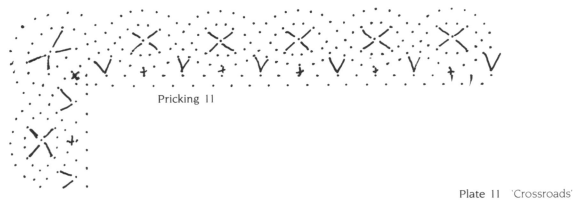

Plate 11 'Crossroads'

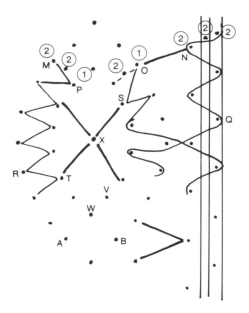

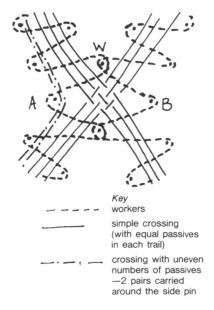

Key
workers

simple crossing
(with equal passives
in each trail)

crossing with uneven
numbers of passives
—2 pairs carried
around the side pin

Fig. 4.1 Working diagram for 'Crossroads'   Fig. 4.2 Enlargement of the crossing

1. Work the trails up to W where we start the multi-crossing. Bring the 2 prs of workers in to the centre, W, and link them with (wh. st.; 2 twists each pr; pin; wh. st.; no twists). Take the l.h. pr out through 4 prs to A and the r.h. pr out through 2 prs to B. Where the numbers of passives in both trails are equal the workers link at W (or any equivalent point), then each worker goes out to its side pin hole (A and B in both Figs. 4.1 and 4.2).

2. The passive prs on each side are worked through each other as in the first half of a spider. Take the 2 centre prs and decide on one side as your workers, say the r.h. pr. Work wh. st. through the 2 prs on the l.h. side, similarly take the second pr on the r.h. side and work through the 2 l.h. prs, but *not* through the original workers; it is always '2 prs through 2 prs', '3 prs through 3 prs', etc.

3. Complete the crossing by bringing the workers from each side (which were left at A and B), through the prs on their respective side; work

them with (wh. st.; 1–2 twists; pin; wh. st.; no twist) and the basic crossing is complete.

In the particular pattern we are working, though, the number of pairs on each side is unequal; this is nearly always the case when crossing a headside trail with an inner trail. Basically the crossing is identical to that described above, but where there is an unequal number of passives, the crossing is made with the smaller number—in 'Crossroads' with 2 prs; the additional prs (2 here) on the headside trail are just carried around the side pin, A, to come back into the trail immediately the crossing is complete. Fig. 4.2 will explain both the simple crossing and that used in 'Crossroads'.

The corner

4. The corner should present no problems, but note that the actual corner hole on the footside has to be used twice to accommodate the kiss which is needed to link the inner trail to the footside.

Kangaloon

This pattern introduces the typically Cluny way of crossing 2 pairs of bobbins from one plait or tally through and across the trail and out from it on the opposite side. Careful arrangement of the pinholes is needed—or a careful reading of the pattern—but the finished result is worth the time taken on these preliminaries.

The main advantage of using this method to link plaits or tallies with a trail is that the density of the trail remains constant, as can be seen in all the trails in this piece of lace except the headside trail. While this method is not actually used in Bedfordshire or Maltese lace I can see no argument against its use in a modern inter-pretation of an old pattern or in a contemporary design where the other features (such as the square-ended tallies) indicate that this is a Bedfordshire-Maltese design.

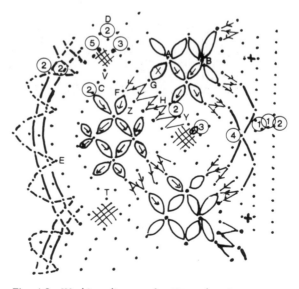

Fig. 4.3 Working diagram for 'Kangaloon'

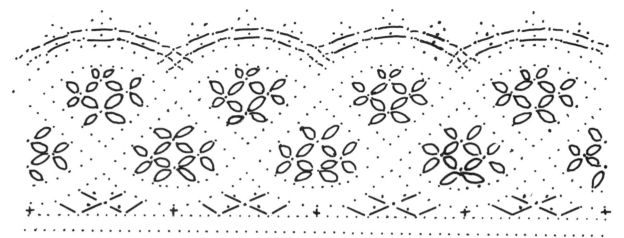

Pricking 12

Plate 12 'Kangaloon'

Materials: 34 prs of bobbins wound in No. 80 linen lace thread; Belgian thread was used in the sample shown in Plate 12.

To Work

The footside and headside should present no problems; note the double row of parallel plaits, each with a single picot, on the headside. Throughout, either single or double picots can be used.

The trails and filling are worked as a single unit. Your position of starting will depend on the end use of the lace; if you intend to join it, the usual rule of starting on the diagonal as far as possible applies. If you want a straight end, start at the top of the pricking, hanging on pairs for the tallies at A and B, the prs for the crossing trails at D, and the prs for the headside plaits and for the footside as indicated on the working diagram, Fig. 4.3. If starting on the diagonal, hang on and add

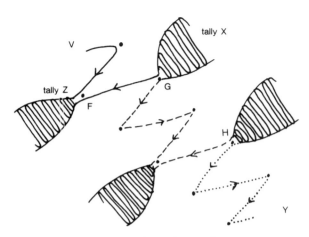

Fig. 4.4 Passing pairs through a trail

prs as in the working diagram. Work a trail crossing, starting from D as in 'Crossroads', noting that 3 prs cross through 3, and 2 prs are carried around the l.h. side. Start the plaited heading and the headside trail, and work to E adding in 2 prs at C.

1. Start the straight trail from V to Y (refer Fig. 4.4) and work to F. At this point twist the workers once or twice; pin in F, then the workers are left here. Go across to the tally X; if not already there,

put a pin between the 2 prs in G or hang 2 new prs on a pin in G. *Take the l.h. pr in wh. st. through the 3 passive prs of the trail; twist once or twice and leave them. You now have 2 prs ready to work tally Z. The second pr from tally X becomes the 'new' workers for the trail.**

A second 'passing of threads' through the trail is worked, as from * to ** above, bringing in or adding in 2 new prs at H; then the whole block of filling can be worked.

2. Return to the heading and headside trail, and complete the crossing, where you will have 8 prs in all, to be crossed with 3 prs from the straight trail Y to T. This will mean that 3 prs will be crossed through 3 prs; 4 prs carried around the corner, and the remaining pair will be the workers.

Note You will have noticed that at the start we had only 6 prs in the headside trail and 2 prs were added in at C. While we always aim to keep the density of the trail at each pattern repeat uniform, the addition of these 2 prs after the start reduces clutter at the first crossing, and the density of the trail from the crossing to point C is slightly increased to make it appear uniform when the final ends are sewn in. Remember that rules are there to be broken when appropriate!

Estelle

In this pattern we further use the technique of passing threads through a trail, and here the use of this technique permits a divided trail to be used. This both adds interest to the pattern and increases the width of the trail without needing to add in extra pairs. This can be seen most clearly in the pricking or working diagram.

Materials: 32 prs of bobbins wound in No. 80 linen lace thread or equivalent; the sample (Plate 13) was worked in Zwicky silk sewing thread, size 50/2. You will also need 4 additional prs for the corner.

To Work
Hang bobbins as indicated on the working diagram, Fig. 4.5; most will be hung on in prs, but on the footside and headside, and where tallies go immediately from the trail (A and B), it is better to hang the bobbins in V-form.

Start at the footside and work to the first kiss; the footside can be either plain or twisted but the latter gives more contrast in a piece of lace which is dominated by wh. st.

So much for the clear-cut part! The two central trails, linked with kisses, 2 prs of tallies which form

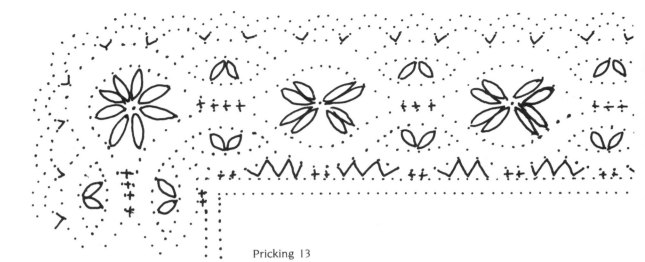

Pricking 13

Plate 13 'Estelle'

a V and the portion of the short curved trails (from C to D and from E to G) have to be worked in together. It is probably best to start with the 2 central trails, linking them with kisses and immediately leaving out 2 prs on the outer edge of each trail for the tallies. These when worked are linked into the short trails, and then the second tally on each side is worked to bring the pairs back into the main trail. Throughout this piece of lace you can decide which method of V-join to use, but try to keep to your initial decision; I had a preference for 1. (p.17) at J and K, and 2. (p.19) at all other places. There is no definite right or wrong; whatever you decide, providing you can justify it, is right.

You will notice that 2 prs leave the trail at B,

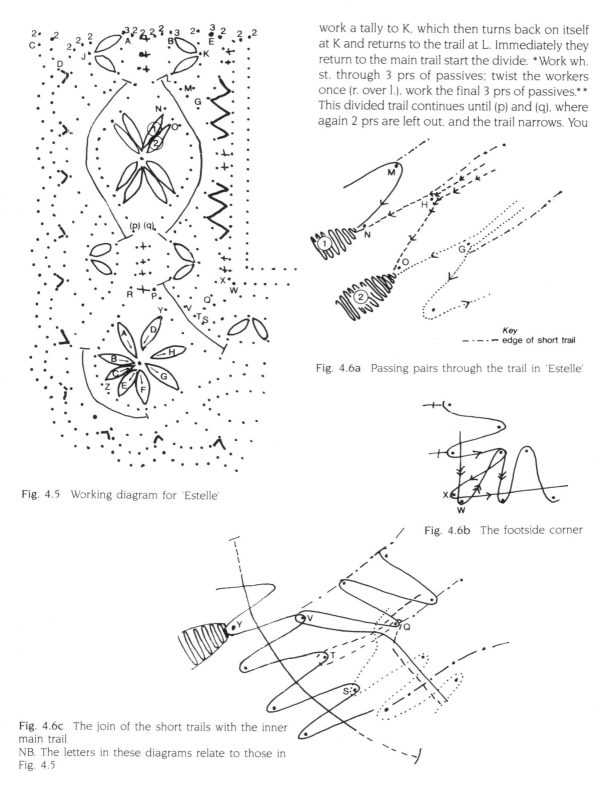

work a tally to K, which then turns back on itself at K and returns to the trail at L. Immediately they return to the main trail start the divide. *Work wh. st. through 3 prs of passives; twist the workers once (r. over l.), work the final 3 prs of passives.** This divided trail continues until (p) and (q), where again 2 prs are left out, and the trail narrows. You

Key
— · — · — edge of short trail

Fig. 4.6a Passing pairs through the trail in 'Estelle'

Fig. 4.6b The footside corner

Fig. 4.5 Working diagram for 'Estelle'

Fig. 4.6c The join of the short trails with the inner main trail
NB. The letters in these diagrams relate to those in Fig. 4.5

will need to concentrate to keep the 'divides' correct; it is all too easy to go gaily along either with or without a divide, only to realise that the change to or from a divide should have been made rows back! Similarly, do not overlook the plaits which link the footside with the small curved trail, nor the heading with the trails on the headside.

The only other part which will need explanation is the conclusion of the short trails and the start of the tallies. Basically the method used is the same as that of passing the threads through the trail used in 'Kangaloon', but here we are short of pin holes as compared with those in 'Kangaloon', so a small adjustment has to be made. Refer to Figs. 4.5 and 4.6a; at N the tally (1) is worked with the original workers from the main trail (M) and the l.h. pr from the short curved trail. The second pr from the short trail (leaving it at H), become the 'new workers', but because of the missing pin hole they only weave through the main trail passives, then go right out from O as the l.h. pr for tally 2; pr 3 from the short trail is the second pr for tally 2, (G–O), and the final pr from the short trail becomes the 'new workers'—G to Q, etc.

The l.h. trails are worked similarly, with the prs from the l.h. short trail passing through the main trail to work the 2 upper r.h. tallies.

The tallies in this arrangement, being grouped in definite pairs, need to be on the skinny side; if yours tend to be wider you may have to work at them a bit. The tallies are crossed in the centre with an eight-plait crossing.

The corner

We are still working simple corners, and only 4 extra pairs are needed for this corner!

The corner really starts at R and P where an extra kiss is worked to link the 2 main trails. Continue with the outer trail and heading, working to the point where the first tally starts. The pairs for this are passed through the trail as before; the second pr from the short trail does not, however, go through the trail but goes *into* the trail so that you gain 2 prs and the trail increases marginally in width; these 2 prs will leave the trail to work tally B. As soon as these 2 prs leave the trail, and you thus have a static

number of pairs in the trail for a portion of it, re-start the divided trail, continuing it until the pairs from the tally F rejoin the trail. At Z add in 2 prs to work the third tally, C.

Looking at the rest of the corner, we need 2 further prs to be added in at Y for tally D, and then we can continue with the footside and main trail, noting when the trail divides and rejoins. The footside corner follows the pattern already established of changing over workers and passives, and using the corner pin twice, as in Fig. 4.6b. The working of the portion of the short trails where they link with the inner main trail is best followed from the working diagram, Fig. 4.6c. The original workers provide the first link, then become passives; the inner passives become workers to go to the second link pin T; after using the central pin Q a second time they become passives again. The third link pin, S, is worked with the inner central pair of passives, and they continue as the new workers.

Having completed the lace up to, and just after, the exact corner you can now complete the corner by working each of the trails in turn, adding in the prs from tallies E, F, G and H as indicated, and throwing out 2 prs from the main trails (to compensate for those added in) when the trails become sufficiently dense to prevent the cut ends running back.

Notes

1. The original pattern as described above produces a light, open lace. Should you wish to use the lace on an article which needs frequent washing or which calls for a slightly more substantial lace, the eight-petalled flower with 8 pr crossing can be replaced with 8 shorter petals and a central half stitch bud, as in the centre of 'Marguerite', *except* that the plaits will be arranged in pairs as in the main pattern and the holes for the central half stitch bud will need rearrangement.

2. The term 'divided trail' is used in many different ways, that described above being only one. In Cluny lace the term is used to describe a trail worked entirely in double stitch (wh. st.; twist—workers and passives once) and yet other lacemakers use the term to describe a single trail which splits into two trails.

1. A child's dress trimmed with 'Helianthus' (page 22)

2. A coffee-table cloth edged with 'Glifada' (page 33). Note the unusual size; the lace was made the exact size of the table so that it sits on top of the table, and thus shows up better than when the lace hangs over the edge

3. The Maltese
collar 'Combine'
(page 112)

4. The round mat, 'Venus' (page 38), protecting the table under the vase of tulips, while the bookmark, 'Georgina' (page 58) waits to be used

5 Further links—bars

So far we have used two methods of linking various parts of the pattern—plaits and tallies. Two further methods are explored in this chapter, *twisted bars*, consisting of a single pair of threads, and the so-called *Venetian bar*. The latter is more closely allied to the tally than to the simple twisted bar; however, being called a bar it is included here. Both these bars occur more frequently in the Cluny version of this lace than in Bedfordshire. The first piece of lace is a round mat; it was originally designed to replace the paper lace in a small double-sided glass tray, as seen in Colour Plate 7, but it would be equally suitable for any small decorative panel; the twisted bars are introduced here.

The second piece of lace, 'Coogee Beach', features the Venetian bar.

Ring-a-Ring o' Roses

This piece of lace can be worked as a single unit, requiring a large number of bobbins, and a large pillow to support them, or in two parts. If you choose the latter, the two outer trails and the two circlets of half stitch buds will be worked in the first part, and the centre whole stitch circlet, zig-zag of plaits and central bud will be worked as the second part. The materials used will depend on the method you choose to work the motif; the motif shown in Colour Plate 7 was worked in two parts, the sample illustrated in Plate 14 was worked in one piece.

Materials: For the motif worked in two parts you will need 32 prs of bobbins wound in DMC Brillante No. 30; the second portion will need approximately 18 of these pairs either rewound or, more likely, rejoined, using thread which is left on the bobbins. You will need fine pins, and enough pricking card to prick the whole circle motif to avoid the need to move up.

Preparation: Either photocopy or trace the pattern, and prepare a complete pricking. (N.B. Please re-read the note on p.25 regarding photocopying.)

To Work
Turn to the working diagram, Fig. 5.1, and note that extra pin holes need to be made in the two trails at A and B. As is usual in laces in this family, several parts of the pattern have to be worked in together, so although the total number of pairs of bobbins to be hung on at the start will be indicated, I would not expect them all to be hung on at once, but to be added as you come to that

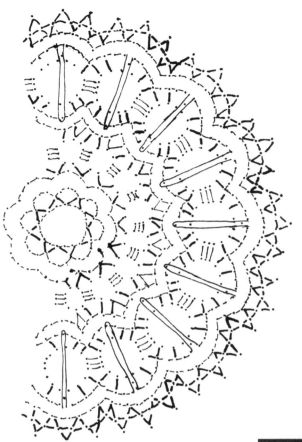

Pricking 14

part of the lace. Starting from the outside, hang 2 prs of bobbins at each of the pins J and I for the heading; 2 prs at each of the pins L, A and M for the outer trail; 2 prs at each of the pins C, N, G and H, and 1 pr each from pins D, E and F for the outer bud; finally, you will need 2 prs each from pins B, O and P for the inner trail.

1. Start with the outer bud; this will be worked entirely in half stitch, with one small exception. Using the 2 prs hanging from pin C, cover the pin with a half stitch, then work through the 3 prs hanging from pins D, E and F, and bring in the 2 prs hanging from G, then those from N and H. Work back to Q; put up this pin in the normal fashion and leave the bud with this pin uncovered. Note that in future repeats each of the pairs which were brought in at C, G, H and N will come from plaits.

2. Now turn to the outer trail, which is worked in conjunction with the plaited heading. Work the trail and heading to K, adding in prs as already indicated. From K work through the 5 prs of passives, then twist the workers approximately 5 times to cover the distance between the outer trail and the half stitch bud. Work (wh. st.; twist) through the original workers from the bud which

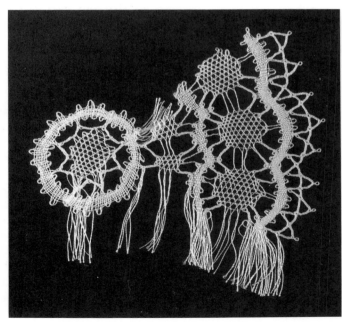

Plate 14 A portion of 'Ring-a-Ring o'Roses'

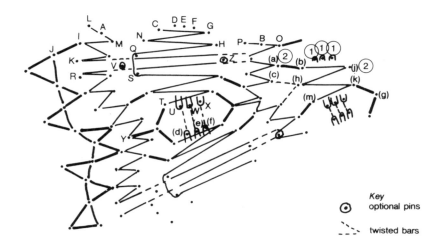

Fig. 5.1 Working diagram for 'Ring-a-Ring o'Roses'

were left at Q, then half stitch through all but the last pr of passives of the bud; work this in (wh. st.; twist). Twist the workers to reach the inner trail, and link the workers of this trail with the main workers (wh. st.; 2 twists each pr; pin). Take the original outer trail workers back to R, repeating the twists, whole stitches and half stitches as on the outward journey. Work a couple of rows of the outer trail to stabilise the workers, then return to the outer bud. Find the original workers which were left at Q, and which have since worked two wh. sts. with the workers from the outer trail. Put up a pin in S under the workers; cover the pin by working a 1/2 st. with the first pr of passives, then finish the bud, leaving out prs for the plaits where indicated, and finishing with the workers at T. You will now have 3 prs left unaccounted for; put a pin between the 2 threads of each pr in holes U, W and X, and twist each pr to reach pins (d), (e) and (f). Note the 2 pin holes at V and Z; these optional pins are just for support if wanted.

Return to the outer trail and heading, and continue to work—you will determine how far you choose to go, allowing space to work the plaits; when you reach pin Y you will need to use it twice, and at this point you link in the prs from the plait started at T in a U-join.

The inner trail is linked to the small circle of half stitch buds with a plait from (a) to (b) and with a twisted pr from (c) to (h). This bud is

worked from (b) to (m), the three twisted prs linking the two adjoining buds in the circlet being treated as those in the larger bud.

3. At this point your work will be determined by your initial choice of method of working. If you decide to work the pattern in two parts you will work a plait from (k) to (g), give one extra twist to the r.h. pr of the plait, then plait on to the next bud. If you elect to work the whole pattern in one piece you will need to start the central trail, following the working diagram, Fig. 5.2, and

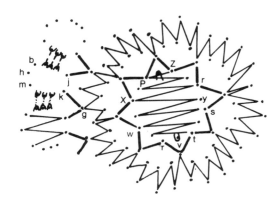

Fig. 5.2 The central portion of 'Ring-a-Ring o'Roses'

having four pairs of passives and one pr of workers for this trail. The plaits linking this trail with the inner buds will then be joined into the trail with a V-join as you come to the appropriate place. At the same time the central half stitch bud will be started so that the linking plaits from the central trail can be worked as you come to them.

4. Whichever method you have chosen to work, the central bud is worked in the same way. Following Fig. 5.2 again, hang 2 prs from a pin placed at (z), and add in 1 pr at each succeeding pin hole of the bud until you reach (y); you should now have 9 prs of bobbins in the bud. At (x), in addition to adding in a new pr, you will link in the plait from the inner trail, probably with a V-join. At each pin after (y) you will need to leave out a pr, and the way in which you will do this will depend on the position of the pin in the pattern. If no prs are left out at the pin for a plait, the pr is just left out to be sewn in afterwards. If a plait goes from the pin to the trail as at (w), the pr can be 'lost' in the plait by adding in the pr and working the plait with 6 threads, 2 single threads and 2 prs of threads, counting each of these double prs as a single thread. When you have worked 2–3 half stitches one of these extra threads can be thrown out; these threads can be just cut off, as the firmness of the plait will hold the cut ends adequately. When the central bud is finished you will have 7 prs of threads which have been left out and so far not dealt with, including the two final prs from (v); five of these will have to be sewn in later, but the remaining 2, at (t) and (s), can be added in to their respective plaits, as at (w). The linking plaits will have to be sewn in to the central bud at (r), (z) and (p).

5. If you elect to work the mat in two portions the central trail, linking plaits and central bud will be worked exactly as described above, and in addition sewings will be taken into each of the pin holes left when the plaits on the right of the smaller buds were worked, and the corner turned.

To complete
Either finish off the first part of the mat, taking sewings into the starting pin holes, then rejoining the bobbins and working the second portion, finishing off with sewings as before, or finish off the entire mat. If the mat is to be mounted, the prs should be knotted with a reef knot, and the ends then taken through the mounting material and finished off on the reverse side. If you are to insert the lace between glass you will need to sew the ends back into the work very carefully so that the join is as invisible as possible. You should have no problem with this by now!

Coogee Beach
(pronounced 'kujee')

The main features of this pattern are the Venetian bars which outline the shape of the breaking wave on the sand mound. While the sample shown in Plate 15 was worked in white, the lace in this pattern is particularly suitable for colour work, picking up the colours of the sea and sand.

Materials: 20 prs of bobbins wound in either No. 80–90 linen lace thread, or No. 30 Brillante d'Alsace (DMC); 2 single bobbins, each with a long neck if possible, wound as full as can comfortably be managed—these are the weavers for the bars, and they use a lot of thread, approximately 3 m for the sample shown in Plate 15; 2 prs of bobbins wound in No. 8 pearl, the supports for the bars.

To Work
Hang bobbins as indicated on the working diagram, Fig. 5.3, having 1 pr No. 8 pearl and one of the single bobbins at each of the pins A and B.

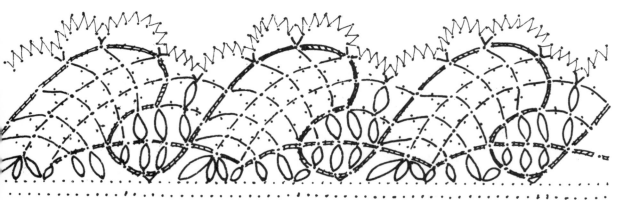

Pricking 15

Plate 15 'Coogee Beach'

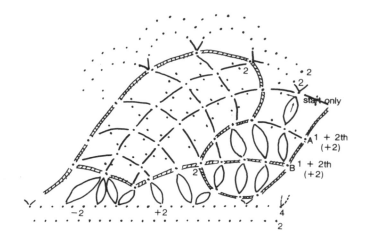

Fig. 5.3 The start of 'Coogee Beach'

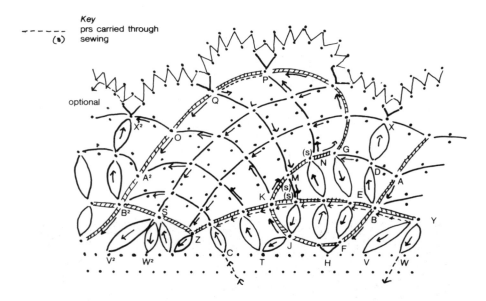

Key
- - - - - prs carried through
(s) sewing

Fig. 5.4 Working diagram for the pattern 'Coogee Beach'

The footside is a plain one, having a basic 2 prs of passives, but starting with 4 prs to keep the pattern correct; 2 of these prs will go out into a tally at C.

1. Start the 'wave' bar at A. The two thick threads (No. 8 pearl) will be the supporting threads, and the single thread the weaver; the latter starts to the right of the supports. Numbering the supports 1 and 2 and following Fig. 5.3 *weave over no. 2, under no. 1, around and over no. 1, and under no. 2. Carefully ease the weaver up into position,** determining the width of the bar from this first round of weaving. Repeat from * to ** until the bar reaches from pin A to just short of pin B on the working diagram, Fig. 5.4, allowing the bar to curve slightly. You are aiming for either a completely straight, or where appropriate, slightly curved, firm bar; I find this is best achieved by keeping the 2 supports fairly close together at all times, and strictly parallel, and by easing the weaver into position after each round.

2. At B add in bobbins for the second Venetian bar with a windmill crossing—this will be worked with 2 'threads', each consisting of 1 heavy and 1 working weaving thread, and 2 'threads' of single heavy threads. If you look carefully at both Plate 15 and Fig. 5.3 you will see that 2 more prs

are needed at B, but until you are familiar with the Venetian bar it is best to cross these, and to add the 2 prs for the tally from B to D with sewings. Work the bars from B to E and from B to F.

3. The plaited filling with picots (mostly on both sides of each plait, but note the exceptions where you have only a single picot), and the tallies should present no problems if you follow the directional arrows carefully. The footside has already been described, and the headside is a typical Cluny heading.

We can therefore concentrate on the Venetian bars and the crossings. The bars in future will be called the 'wave' and the 'sandhill', the latter being the bar from Y to Z. Sew 2 prs into the starting pin hole at A, and 2 into the hole at B, and start the filling, all crossings being windmills except those to be described. At G give the l.h. pr of the plait 1–2 extra twist(s); pin; and then use the same 2 prs to work the tallies from G to E, from E to F, and the plait from F to H. The crossings at both E and F are windmills, worked with the 2 prs from the tally, 1 single gimp thread, and 1 × (1 gimp and the weaver from the bar). The majority of crossings will either be of this variety or the crossing of 2 bars as described for the crossing at B. The short plait from F to H will be linked to the footside with your choice of V-join, and these prs will work right through to P, but stopping for the present at N. Continue the wave bar to J; put up a pin with 1 extra twist to the outer (r.h.) pr; work the bar to K; windmill crossing with the sandhill bar, which likewise has an empty pin hole, and bring the wave bar around to M (where you again have an empty pin hole), to N (windmill crossing with the prs from the tally) and to G. Here take a sewing into the empty pin hole left when the plait turned into a tally.

The wave bar is continued as described above, and as shown in the working diagram. Start the Cluny heading where indicated on the working diagram, and work it in with the bars, plaits and tallies.

Basically we now have two further problems; there are several multiple crossings, each needing different treatment because of the relative positions of the plaits, tallies and bars, and secondly there are two places in the pattern where pairs need to be either carried through, or taken out and rejoined later.

The multiple crossings

1. As the six prs at P cross directly through each other, plait into plait and bar into bar, a normal 6-plait crossing can be worked (see p.16 if necessary).

2. Similarly at Q a 6-plait crossing can be worked (see note below regarding pr 3).

3. The crossings at B and S cause greater problems as the bars and plaits (or tallies) do not cross directly opposite. At both of these crossings work a windmill crossing with the 2 l.h. prs; put the pin up in the usual way, then work a windmill with the 2 r.h. prs, taking out and replacing the pin in the centre of the second windmill, and being very careful to pull it all up firmly (especially the second windmill), without losing the shape of the bars.

4. At O the crossing is a windmill with the 2 r.h. prs only.

Pairs in the wrong place

A. As already stated, 2 prs work the plaits, tallies, and then plaits right through to P, but these prs are then redundant. They are, however, needed to work the plaits and tally from Q to T, and can quite happily be carried from P to Q along with the pearl-supporting threads of the bar, each support then being (1 pr of threads and 1 heavy thread). You will need to slightly adjust the spacing and tension of the bar to keep it uniform, but this raises no problems. The plaits from Q to T will be joined to the bars at M, L and J with sewings.

B. 4 prs from two tallies starting at S come into the footside at V and W; these add too much bulk to the footside. At the same time 2 prs are needed at C to work the plaits through to B^2, so it is necessary to throw out 2 prs in the footside between W and H, and to rejoin them and add them in again at C.

C. We find ourselves again with 2 extra prs at X, and here there are 4 options:

(i) work them into the headside or plait for a short distance, then throw them out (at 2 separate places).

(ii) Work them into the heading, so that you have 4 inner prs of passives, pulling all as firmly as you can—this was done in the 2nd pattern repeat in Plate 15.

(iii) Work them into the plait, thereby working the plait with 4 double threads, again pulling firmly.

(iv) Add 2 prs to the heading and 2 prs to the plait, thus spreading the additional density. In all cases the crossing at O is worked as 4. above.

You should have no further problems, and enjoy the variety which a Venetian bar can add to your work. You will have further opportunities to use it during the course of this book, and then you will be able to add it to your own patterns when you are ready to start designing.

6 Circles and ovals

There are several ways of working both circles and ovals. To a certain degree these methods overlap, as might be expected. In this chapter we look at two basic methods of overcoming the problems associated with working these two shapes; in addition, we look at a well known feature of Bedfordshire lace in particular—an oval bud with a divided centre.

Georgina

Bookmarks provide a good opportunity to learn a new technique (or several new techniques!) and to produce a worthwhile article without spending dozens of hours on it! Make one as a treat for yourself—your book will be all the more enjoyable with a thing of beauty to mark your page—or to give away to a special friend.

Having mastered the techniques of starting on the straight and finishing to a point, you may well be able to adapt some of the other patterns given here to bookmark patterns, insertions naturally being the easiest.

In addition to the new method of starting and finishing, this pattern introduces the oval bud with divisions down the centre, known in parts of Australia, and in some other lace centres, as a 'beetle bud'.

Materials: 50 prs of bobbins wound in No. 60 linen lace thread, or any equivalent firm thread; in this case I feel that linen is by far the best thread to use as it gives to the finished article a crispness which is needed if it is not to be mounted. Coloured linen lace thread from Sweden is occasionally available, or you can dye your own thread if you wish to work the bookmark in colour. As there are a large number of bobbins used, many of which are added in where you need them, it is best not to have them hanging from pins right from the start, but rather to add the bobbins when you reach the appropriate pin hole. Have them ready in a bobbin bag or hanging from a bobbin stand (a mug tree makes an ideal bobbin hanger); do *not* hang the spare prs from the pins waiting to be used in your work, nor around the edge of the pillow, as both get in the way of the portion of the design that you are working.

To Work

Referring to Fig. 6.1, start at A and hang 4 prs of bobbins in V-form, numbering them from the left 1, 2, 3, 4. In whole stitch work (4 through 3; 1 through 2 and 3 through 2). These 4 prs become the workers for the upper border (and later the

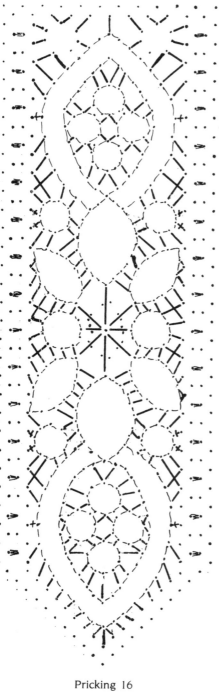

Pricking 16

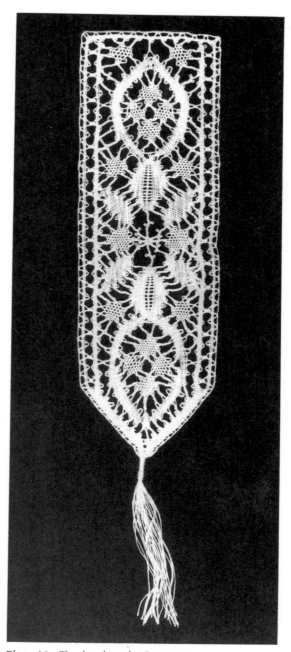

Plate 16   The bookmark 'Georgina'

59

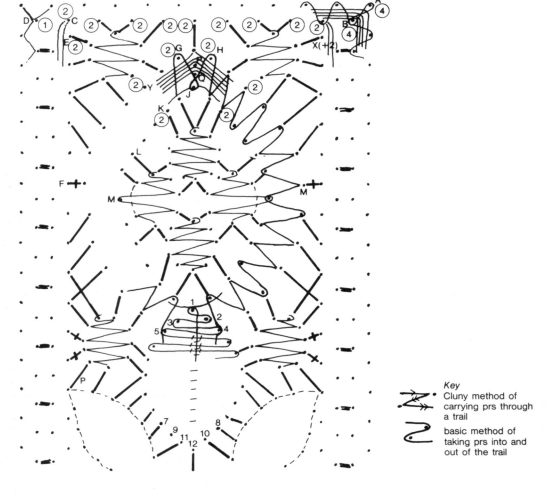

Fig. 6.1 Working diagram for the start of 'Georgina'

Key
Cluny method of carrying prs through a trail

basic method of taking prs into and out of the trail

l.h. footside) and the r.h. footside. Twist the 2 outer prs 2–3 times and the inner prs once.

1. Add 4 prs at B, hanging them on in V-formation, letting the workers lie between the corner pairs and the pin at B. Bring the 2 inner prs of workers (one from each side of the original 4 prs) through 2 prs on the outer, r.h. side and 3 prs on the inner, l.h. side, in wh. st. With the 2 workers make a wh. st.; the r.h. worker is left at B to work the r.h. footside, while the l.h. worker continues to work the upper border. Leave the inner corner pr to become part of the inner cucumber trail later.

2. The footside is a plain one with a straight edge, two prs being added in at each of the inner pins, and left out straight away; these prs will be used to work plaits to join the footside to the top corner buds and to the main oval shape; it is your choice whether you work the plaits (leg) as soon as the prs are added in or when you need them. At C you have 2 options for the start of the inner cucumber trail; you can either add in 3 prs here, one for the workers and 2 for the passives of the trail, or you can add the usual 2 prs to become the passives and a further pr at E for the workers.

The inner corner pin hole will need to be used twice; the first time twist your workers once only, and the second time twist them twice. At this stage you should have 26 prs on your work.

Cucumber trail

3. * Now start the inner cucumber trail on the left, adding in a single pr for the workers at pin D and 2 prs at pin E. Having worked the cucumber (refer to the pattern 'Venus' if necessary), leave the trail, and work the top left hand bud in half stitch, following the direction of the workers as shown on the working diagram, Fig. 6.1. When starting the bud I find that the best result is obtained by taking pr no. 2 (from the left or right, according to the direction of the workers, remembering that you have to work a row before putting up the first pin). Finish each bud in this pattern by working a half stitch with the 2 central pairs; this positions your pairs correctly for the plaits which follow.**

4. You can now start the outer cucumber trail and logically work the whole cucumber edging as far as F, but in practice it is better not to get too far ahead with any one part. I would leave it after the second tally, and work the second portion when needed to work the kiss.

5. Repeat from * to ** on the right hand bud, reversing the direction of the workers on the bud, but still taking no. 2 pr as your workers. Do not forget to add in 1 pr at B and 2 prs at X to work the inner footside.

The upper oval and central bud

6. Work (or check on), the central plait from the top border. Start at the top point of the oval trail by putting a pin between the 2 prs of the plait, allowing one pr to lie at each side of the trail for the passives. Add in 2 prs each at G and H, and hang 2 prs around each of the pins P and Q. Take the 2 upper prs and work through the central prs (as in Fig. 6.1); cross the 2 prs in (wh. st.; twist × 2; pin; cover the pin) and leave, to become the third pr of passives, and then staying in the centre to go into the plait, Cluny fashion, as in 'Kangaloon' (Chapter 4). The outer 2 prs become workers, each in turn working through their respective 3 prs of passives and then staying in the centre to go into the plait, again Cluny fashion. Now work on the l.h. side only, bringing

in 2 prs from the top bud, and leaving out 2 prs on each side for the central bud. Add in 2 prs at Y and K as shown on the working diagram. Work to the kiss on this side, then to the same point on the r.h. side#. In order to keep the trails sufficiently dense, wherever it is possible (i.e. by the positioning of the plaits coming and going out of the trail), I work the Cluny method of passing prs through the trail, so at J, K and L and the rest of the pins on that side I use this method.

7. Work the top bud of the 4, and the 2 side buds as far as the central point of each. Here the workers are taken out through the edge pr, working a (wh. st. and twist) with this pair.

8. Complete the trails and buds as you have the appropriate prs ready to use. You may choose to add in a further 2 prs at M, and on the corresponding point on the other side; this will depend on the density of the trail that you prefer.##

Repeat from # to ## for the r.h. side. Complete the buds, plaits and trails to the lower end. Twist each pr at the end of the trails twice.

The upper central bud and cucumber edgings should need no further explanation; they are worked as the necessary pairs become available.

The oval bud with the divided centre

a. Make sure that the twists from the trails are in place. Start the bud at the apex and work in wh. st.; the inner pr from each trail works the first stitch, and the pr from the r.h. trail becomes the workers for the bud. Work the first five pins (including the apex pin), bringing in 2 prs from each trail at pins (2), (3), (4) and (5). Now start the central division. Find the central pr, and when the workers reach it, give them one twist before working it. Work (wh. st.; twist) with the central pr, then finish the row in wh. st. Work the complete bud with the central division until the complete bud with the central division until you reach the last seven pins; at this point start to close up the central division by leaving the workers on either side of the central pr untwisted, and then on the next row leave out the twists altogether. As you will probably not have enough prs to work each plait to link with the leaves, add in 2 further prs on each side at pins (7) and (8). Leave out (3 × 2) prs for the plaits on either side, giving you 4 prs at the bottom pin. Two of these work the lower left hand plait, and two the central straight plait.

Notes

1. You will have observed that the snatch pin on each side of the lower half of the bud is in a different position; this is purely aesthetic—it looks very much better this way than having the plaits leaving the bud at exactly the same point.

2. Very often, and perhaps one should say more often, particularly in the old laces, the central division in the bud consists of a single row of twisted threads rather than the arrangement we used here. As we work in pairs, starting with an even number (2 or 4), one of which becomes a worker, the central division must be pushed very slightly off centre. This can clearly be seen in many old pieces of lace, where the pairs of bobbins are added in symmetrically; hence my choice of the double twist here.

3. The four leaves should present no problems; the leaf is started with 2 prs from plait R (Fig. 6.1) which also links it with the footside. Two prs are brought in on the inner edge and left out at the outer edge on each pin, with the exception of pin no. 3, which is a snatch pin (Fig. 6.2). Throw out 2 prs at the lower point.

4. The central star of plaits. Having worked the oval bud, 2 upper side buds and the upper leaves, you are now ready to work the central group of plaits. We have 3 × 2 prs ready for the plaits, but need 2 more to link the side central buds. As it means transferring 2 prs from one side bud to the other it is preferable to add in 2 more prs for the central plaits; these can be left out at a convenient place later on, such as the start of a leaf, or by working a plait with 3 prs of bobbins and leaving out the 2 spare bobbins at different places in the plait. Note that the plaits have picots on either side; make sure that they do not split, and watch the length of the plaits carefully so that they lie perfectly straight and evenly. The crossing is an 8-plait crossing.

Treating each pr. of bobbins as if it were a single bobbin:
(i) Work 1/2 st. with the 2 centre prs;
(ii) Work 1/2 st. with the 2 l.h. prs;
(iii) Work 1/2 st. with the 2 r.h. prs;

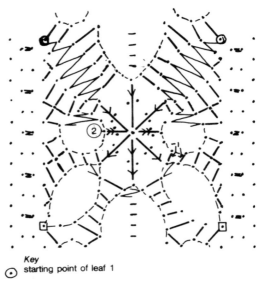

Key
⊙ starting point of leaf 1
□ finishing point of leaf 2

Fig. 6.2 The central part of 'Georgina', showing the working of the leaves and central plaits

(iv), (v) and (vi) Repeat (i), (ii) and (iii);
(vii) Put pin in centre hole, in the centre of the 8 prs; pull up carefully;
(viii) Work wh. st. with the 2 centre prs;
(ix) Take the 6th pr. from the l. and cross it over the 7th pr., i.e. l. over r.—unusually!;
(x) Take the 2nd pr. from the left and cross it over the 3rd pr.—left over right again.

Carefully ease all up into place, and check that your pairs have crossed directly through the centre.

The second half of the bookmark

This should not present any problems until you reach the start of the lower pointed edge. You will need to throw out and add in pairs at appropriate places, but these are techniques with which you are quite familiar by now.

1. At the lower end of the oval bud you should have 14 prs of bobbins before you start to leave prs out—see Fig. 6.3. After twisting twice, these bobbins are left out for the sides of the lower oval in the following order:
(i) l.h. side—2 prs on the second pin from the bottom hole;
(ii) r.h. side—2 prs on the second pin from the bottom hole;

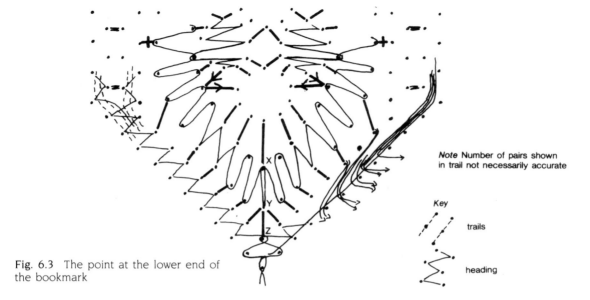

Fig. 6.3 The point at the lower end of the bookmark

Note Number of pairs shown in trail not necessarily accurate

Key

trails

heading

(ii) l.h. side—3 prs on the 1st pin from the bottom hole;

(iv) r.h. side—3 prs on the 1st pin from the bottom hole;

(v) leave 4 prs at the bottom hole, 2 of which, after linking, go to each side.

At the lower end of the final round bud you will have 2 extra prs (as you had 6 plaits coming in to it, but only have 5 going out). Make a plait with 4 prs, gradually throwing out the extra 4 threads.

The lower oval

2. Start working each side from the centre, bringing in the groups of threads left out as above in the correct places. On the r.h. trail you will need to change over your workers to keep the correct line of weaving after the second pin hole.

Finish off the oval by taking in 1 pr on each side from the final central plait. Link the workers at X (Fig. 6.3) and bring them each through the 2 prs of passives on their own side to Y; do not pin up. Cross the 4 remaining prs of passives through each other (as in the first part of a spider); finally cross the workers with (wh. st.; twist × 2; wh. st.) to cover the pin. You should have 6 prs left to work the plaits.

The lower point

3. Working each side in turn, complete the cucumber footside up to and including the last tally.* Take the workers from the footside out to the edge and back through the 2 prs of passives, then leave them inside the passives. The workers from the inner trail become your workers for the combined footside leading to the point. Continue the side of the point, bringing in prs from plaits as they occur, gradually building up the number of pairs in the trail until you are quite satisfied that a cut end can be supported by the density of the fabric. You can then start to leave out prs, always throwing out (to the back of your work) the 2nd pr of passives from the footside, thus keeping the edge pr for a straight line, and throwing out a pr which has been in the footside for the greatest length of time. Continue in this way until you reach Z, aiming to have no more than 8 prs left at this point.** Repeat this move once for the penultimate pins and work the final pin with (wh. st.; twist × 2; pin; wh. st.) to cover the pin.

4. Carefully work 6–10 cm of lace plait, dividing the number of prs you are left with by 4, and finish off with a gathering knot as used in macramé (also called 'whipping' if you have been in the Scout or Guide movements) or with an overhand knot. The gathering knot should be worked with the bobbins still on the threads, but the overhand knot will have to be tied after the bobbins have been cut off.

Alanna

In this pattern we meet oval shapes in a form that is probably familiar to you, although it is sometimes hard to recognise that the circular or oval shapes are in fact identical in method of working to the diamond or square in torchon lace, where the pairs are divided to form two trails or sides. At first sight the pattern may appear very open, but the firm headside and footside and the solid four-leaved clover motif balance the open spaces. The corner, which takes the hardest wear, has deliberately been filled in, but you may like to remove some of the buds and replace them with your own arrangement of plaits (with picots).

Materials: 37 prs of bobbins (maximum) wound in No. 100 linen lace thread, or equivalent cotton thread.

To Work

Choose a suitable starting point on your pattern and decide where you will hang your bobbins; you should have no problems if you start where there are several plaits. The footside has three prs of passives with a snatch pin edge. You will need to carefully work out the number of pairs needed for the headside. First, assess the number you will need to cover the ground at the extreme headside of each curve, then add in all the pairs you will need to take out from the trail. While it is easier to add in the pairs as you need them, in this case it would make the final pattern uneven, as this particular pattern repeat would be thinner in the portion A to B on the working diagram (Fig. 6.4). When working the half stitch bud bring in the new pairs with (half st., wh. st.; twist; pin; half stitch).

There are only two features of the pattern which need explanation, the headside and the four-leaved clover.

The headside

This is a half stitch trail, and as designed it is worked in half stitch with a picot heading. A snatch pin heading could be substituted if preferred. To avoid too much crowding of pins on the inner side of the sharp curve, pins are used twice at D, E and F (on every pattern repeat). At A you will find that you either need to use the inner pin 3 times, or better, use it normally the first time, change over your workers the second time, and choose between the two methods the third time, depending on which gives you the neatest result.

2. In the sample, Plate 17, you will notice 2 different versions of the reversed curve J to A; in the first, the lazy way of working it, all pairs were left in, leaving a *very* thick trail in which the half stitch is totally lost. In the second repeat of this portion (after the corner) pairs were taken out, to be replaced when needed, mostly in the plaits leaving the trail. I am sure you will agree that, although this takes more effort, the result is so vastly superior that it is well worth making the extra effort.

3. Taking out pairs in half stitch, though, does raise some problems, and there is no totally satisfactory way of doing it—if you do know of one, do share it through the pages of your national lace journal. Here I have used the Honiton method: where you intend to take out a pr, work a whole stitch in the row before, preferably just inside the edge pair. On the row itself throw out the 2 centre prs of the whole stitch, knotting them with a reef knot (and *do* make sure it's not a granny!), before laying them to the back of your work.

The four-leaved clover

4. As there seems to be a maze of holes on the pricking I find it helpful sometimes to take a different coloured pen and lightly outline the shape of the motif (as in that immediately after the corner in Fig. 6.4). Start at Z where you have 4 prs coming from the plaits; work in wh. st. from Z to Y. On reaching Y you should have 8 prs; work through 4 prs; pin; work out to X and back through 3 prs to W. Leave this side. On the left side the 4th pr from the left become the workers, which go out to V. Work on both sides in turn, linking the 2 sides where indicated with 2 small tallies, identical in working to those used in a cucumber foot. Two prs are added in at X and

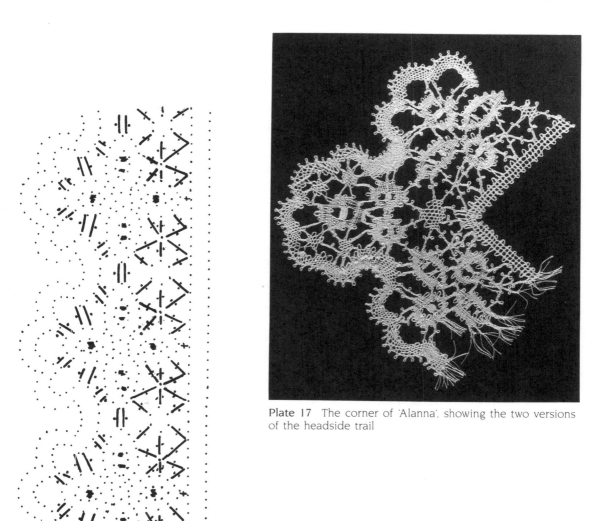

Plate 17 The corner of 'Alanna', showing the two versions of the headside trail

Pricking 17

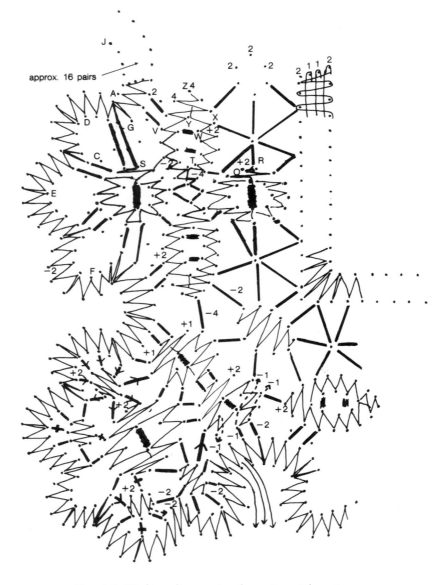

Fig. 6.4 Working diagram for the pattern 'Alanna'

left out immediately to work the plait; throw out 2 prs just before the end of the oval, and at the finish there should be 8 prs left, which are used to work 2 short plaits on each side to link with the side buds.

5. The right oval starts with 2 prs coming from a plait at R; 2 prs are added in at Q. Here the division of prs for the 2 sides is not quite as straightforward as for the first oval, as you need to make allowance for the 4 prs which will be brought in on the l.h. side. Thus, in this oval, after the join 2 prs will be left out for the central tally, 3 prs will go to the l.h. side, and 3 prs to the r.h. side. When bringing the 2 prs from the tally back

5. Motif for a trinket box: 'Lulu'. (p.26)

6. The fan 'Autumn Leaves' (p.138)

67

7. The Maltese square, 'Bizzilla'
(page 118), and 'Ring-a-Ring o'Roses'
(page 51) mounted in a glass tray

8. The Maltese christening gown
made by Josephine Caruana
(see p.110)

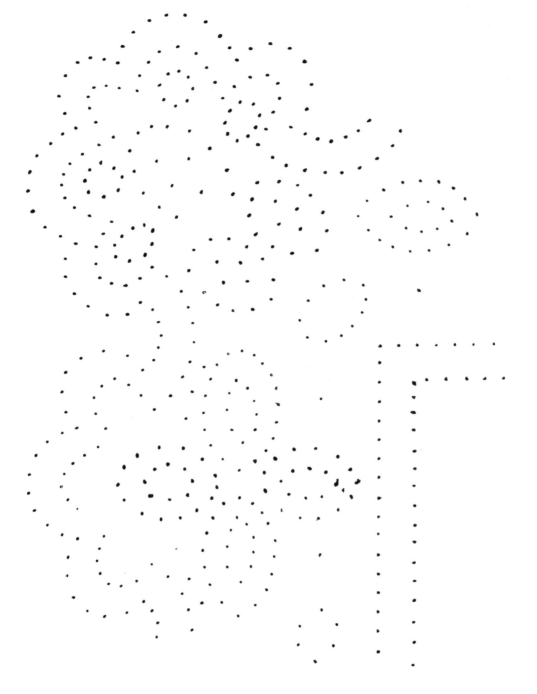

Fig. 6.5 Enlargement (140% of original) for marking in your way of working the corner of 'Alanna'

into the ring, take 1 pr in on each side before working the linking stitch. 2 prs have to be thrown out, or lost in a plait, at the end of this oval.

6. The left oval, however, has 6 prs coming in, and 6 going out, so the division will be central. Start the oval at S.

7. The fourth oval should be quite straightforward; 2 prs will need to be added in to work the first plait out to the l.h. side (as at X) and thus prevent the work from becoming 'starved' (i.e. thin). 2 prs are lost in the lower r.h. plait, and 4 prs in the lower central plait.

8. The corner should present no difficulties if you follow the working diagram (Fig. 6.4) and use your own initiative. Remember, and this is *most* important, that the working diagrams are only meant to be a general guide, and you may well discover a way of working any of the patterns which appeals to you more, or gives a result which you prefer. For this reason an enlarged blank diagram is included for this pattern (Fig. 6.5), on which you can mark the way you finally worked the corner, ensuring, hopefully, that not only are the 4 corners identical, but each pattern repeat bears a nearly complete resemblance to the patterns which precede and follow it. Nowadays most people have access to an enlarging and reducing photocopier, and even if it means enlarging from one enlargement to another, a large version of a pricking can be invaluable in working any pattern other than the most simple.

If you decide to work as suggested for 'Alanna', don't forget to take out pairs in the reverse curve portion, J to A, and to replace them when needed.

On first sight this pattern may appear complicated, but do not be put off; when it is carefully analysed you will see that it really is quite simple, and I can assure you that it *does* grow quite quickly!

Jill

This small motif, suitable for putting under a glass paperweight, in the lid of a trinket box, or for decoration on a dress, introduces the second method of working a circle (or an oval), the first being identical in working to the oval shapes in 'Alanna'. Neither method gives perfect results, and we just have to choose that which is dictated by the pricking or which suits the pattern best. The method used here results in a good circle shape, but it is rather thin at the start and finish; however, I will show you how this can be, to a large measure, avoided.

Materials: 28 prs of bobbins wound in No. 100 linen lace thread, No. 30 Retors d'Alsace (DMC), or Zwicky 'Iris' silk thread.

To Work

Hang bobbins on the starting line as indicated on the working diagram, Fig. 6.6, and start the main half stitch trail. It seems a lot of bobbins

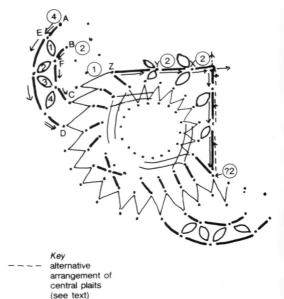

Key
– – – – alternative arrangement of central plaits (see text)

Fig. 6.6 The first quarter of the motif 'Jill'

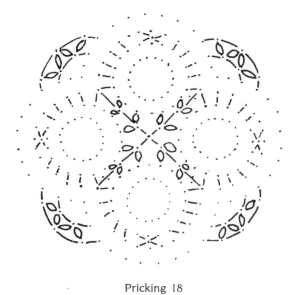

Pricking 18

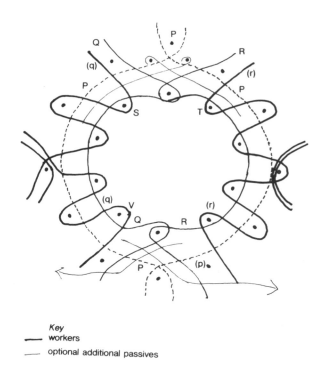

Plate 18 'Jill'

for the start, but remember that we want this pattern repeat to be identical to the other three, and we will need to leave out bobbins from the trail for 7 plaits, the first 4 prs being left out immediately. Work until you reach C, and temporarily leave the trail.

1. Put up pins A and B and hang 4 prs from A and 2 prs from B; work a double plait from A to E—i.e. an ordinary plait, but each pr having 2 threads. Work a single plait from B to F. The two plaits are linked with 4 small petal-shaped tallies, each of which is joined to the relevant plait with a windmill crossing. After working tally no. 4 you will have 4 prs on the outside and 2 on the inside. Work double and single plaits as before.

2. Continue with the main trail, bringing in these 6 prs and leaving out prs where necessary for plaits on the l.h. side. Work a plait with picots where indicated from Z to Y. Join in 2 prs at Y and work a tiny tally to reach the circle, and repeat from X. It may seem rather strange at first working the tallies backwards, but with practice it becomes as easy as in the usual direction.

3. Now turn to the circle and to Fig. 6.7; to work this kind of circle you must have three plaits to come into the circle at adjoining holes, the central one being the starting point; here it is P and the

Key
—— workers
— optional additional passives

Fig. 6.7 Working the circle

71

adjoining plaits are Q and R. The easiest way to learn to work the circle is by following the diagram, but in case you find it easier to follow printed instructions I will also describe the working.

4. Put a pin between the 2 prs of plait P and cover the pin with a wh. st. and leave. These 2 prs become the outer passives of the circle. . . (dotted lines on the diagram). Pin between the prs of plait Q. Take the r.h. pr of plait Q and work wh. st. through the l.h. pr of plait P.

5. Put up a pin between the prs of plait R. Take the r.h. pr of plait R and work wh. st. through pr 2. Work a wh. st. with these 2 prs, Q and R; pin in the centre, and cover with a wh. st.—these 2 prs become the inner passives, the other passives being the 2 prs from P.

6. *Take the l.h. pr from plait Q (q), and work wh. st. through the 2 prs of passives; pin in S; continue with this pr of workers, bringing in prs from the plaits where indicated.** Repeat from * to ** on the r.h. side, using (r) as your workers, and putting up the first pin in T.

7. To finish off the circle, you again need 3 adjacent plaits leaving the circle; # work pin V using (q) as workers; work wh. st. through 2 prs of passives and leave these workers.## Repeat from # to ## on the other side, continuing to use (r) as workers.

Take the 2 outer prs of passives, P and (p), and cross with a wh. st. between the 2 prs, then work a plait with these 2 prs.

This, together with the semi-circular portion already described, completes the first quarter of the pattern, all but the central plaits, starting with 2 of the 4 prs left out at Z. You have already worked the plait to X; work it to the central pin; give each pr 2 twists and put up a pin. Continue with the plait, turning it after a few half stitches have been worked, and continue to work the second central plait out to the trail. The tallies here will come from the circle, and you will have 2 extra prs in the trail; these can be taken out, or left in, giving slight additional thickness on the 2 portions of the trail directly opposite each other.

To complete
8. Take sewings in each of the starting pin holes, and either sew the end in or take the threads through to the back of a piece of mounting fabric, and either knot off there or sew the ends neatly into the fabric if you wish to avoid bulk—depending, of course, on the end use of the motif.

Notes
1. If you find that the circle is too starved at the start, make additional pin holes between P and Q, and P and R, and hang one pr from each of these pins, allowing these extra prs to become passives. They are thrown out at the end as shown in the diagram of the circle, and the ends disposed of as described for the completion above.

2. The central plaits: rather than turning the central plait back on itself and working the second one from the centre to the trail, you may prefer to add in a second pr and work plait no. 2 also from the trail to the centre; the plaits are then crossed with a windmill crossing and plaits 3 and 4 will both go from the centre to the trail; it will be essential to throw out 2 prs after bringing the second 2 prs back into the trail, otherwise it will look really lopsided!

3. I find it helpful to take a careful look at the pricking before starting, and to mark with a coloured pencil a circle around the pin holes and the starting and finishing pin holes of each repeat.

7 Raised tallies

In the pattern 'Hettie' of this chapter we encounter our first piece of Spanish Cluny-type lace. Much of the lace from Spain is needlepoint, but fine 'blonde' lace was made for Church use, and for the delicate mantillas, the national headdress of Spain. Most of this lace was made in convents, while a coarser pillow lace, much of it of the Cluny-style, was made in the homes and used largely for household purposes. The pillows used were long and narrow, similar in style to the traditional Maltese pillow.

Raised tallies are very much a feature of this family of laces, especially in the Bedfordshire lace (where, of course, they are called 'raised plaits'),

and in Cluny lace where the tallies are largely petal-shaped. There are two forms of raised tallies—the first is the raised petal which is just a petal, or group of petals, over which the weaving continues, either in whole stitch or in half stitch, so that the finished result is a flat petal lying on top of the woven shape. The more complicated form of raised tally, at least to work, is the 'bobble'. Here a long plait is worked, then is doubled back over or under itself to form a little raised button.

We will work the petal-shaped tally first, as I think it is the easier of the two, followed by the bobble-shaped tally.

Hettie

This pattern was based on a piece of Spanish lace sent to me by an 86-year old cousin; she wrote, 'I learnt lace-making as a child in El Ferrol, Spain. The nuns who taught me just referred to it as "Pillow lace", perhaps because I was only learning Spanish, and none of them spoke English. It must surely have had a name. The samples, (this and the pattern 'Mollie' on page 98) 'must both be 60 years old: the wide lace edged linen towels and an old-fashioned bed valance.' I have slightly altered the pattern from the original, particularly in replacing very sparse bobble tallies with petal

tallies, which to me make a very great improvement to the design.

Materials: Approximately 50 prs of bobbins, wound in No. 35, 40 or 50 linen lace thread, depending on the density of lace that you prefer, or that which is most suitable for your end use. The sample was worked in No. 35 Swedish linen lace thread.

As all these threads are considerably coarser than those you have been using, remember to well fill—but not overfill—the bobbins to avoid

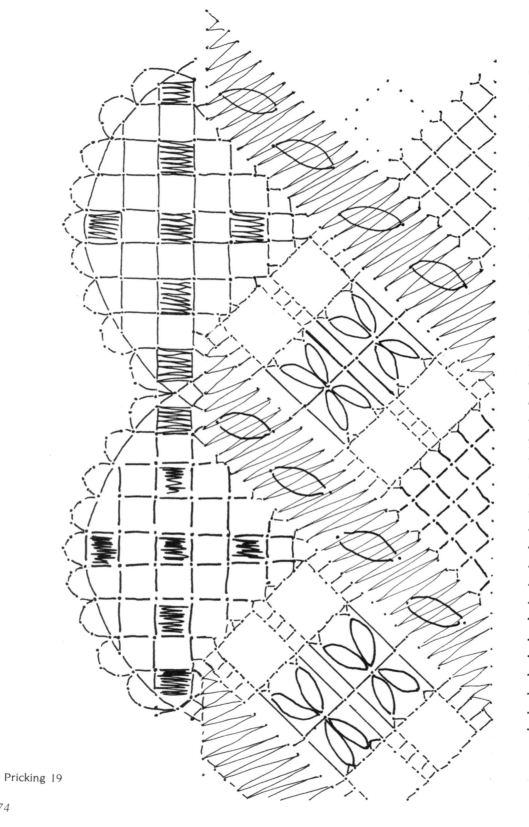

Pricking 19

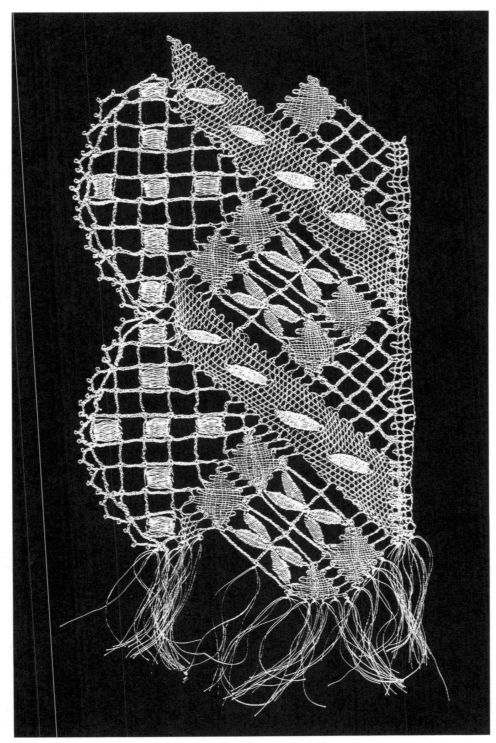

Plate 19   A portion of the Spanish Cluny pattern 'Hettie'

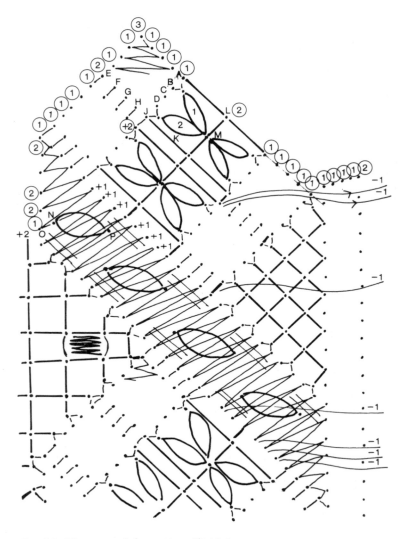

Fig. 7.1 The start of the pattern 'Hettie'

refilling them too often, and to use your largest bobbins!

To Work

Have your bobbins all ready to hang on as you need them, and refer to Fig. 7.1 when starting the main body of this pattern.

1. Start at the top of the whole stitch diamond and add in prs as you come to them, noting that the 3rd pin on the l.h. side is a snatch pin. 2 prs will be left out at each of the pins A and B—or if you prefer you can leave out 3 prs at pin A and 1 pr at pin B. C is a snatch pin; 1 pr is left out

at pins D, E, F, G and H, leaving 4 prs at pin J, one of which goes into tally 2, one into the long half stitch block, and 2 into the plait to K. This pattern is followed, sometimes with slight modifications, in each of the following diamonds and you should by now be able to work out each from this guide.

2. Work the second diamond, then plait A to L. Tally no. 1 is worked with the 2 prs left out at pin B, or if you left out (3 + 1) prs at A and B it will be worked with the l.h. pr from A and the pr from pin B. Tally no. 2 is worked with the r.h. pr from pin J and the pr from pin D. At the conclusion

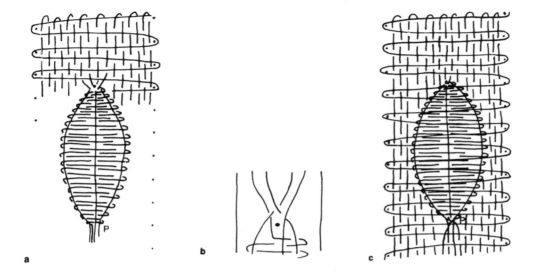

Fig. 7.2 Working a petal-shaped raised tally: a the tally worked, showing the prs taken from the ground; b enlargement of the start of the tally; c bringing the pairs back into the weaving

of these 2 tallies add in 2 prs at L and work a plait to M, working a 6-plait crossing at this point.

3. Work the second group of plaits and tallies similarly, then gently push the bobbins you have used to the right, and have your spare bobbins ready to start the long half stitch block. This is quite straightforward until you reach the start of the raised tally, N.

4. After putting up the pin at O, work half stitch through prs 1 and 2 from the left (or more if you want a heavier block or are using a finer thread), then gently push these to the left. The next two prs will be used to work the raised tally so turn to Fig. 7.2. Work a 1/2 st. with these 2 prs; put up a pin in hole N, then take pr 2 and weave a good petal-shaped tally (essential, as the 3-D effect makes them more visible even than a flat tally, so be prepared to do the tally more than once if you are dissatisfied with the first one!). Work a 1/2 st. at the lower end of the tally and put up a pin at P. Take a small handkerchief, coloured if possible, or a piece of thin cloth of similar size, and cover this tally with it; do not pin it down.

5. Find the main workers, and continue with the 1/2 st. block until you reach P; work through the first two prs of this row (numbered from the right), then remove the cloth which was covering the tally and bring the 2 prs from it back into the 1/2 st. block. Continue with this block, working the 2nd tally similarly, until you reach the start of the 3rd tally, then leave this portion. It is not advisable to get too far ahead in any one part, firstly because it makes working marginally more difficult, and secondly—and more importantly— if you find an error a long way back it is much, much more to undo!

The headside fan

6. Turn now to the headside 'fan' area, and to Fig. 7.3. The figures on this diagram indicate the number of prs used to work that particular portion, e.g. (1) = a twisted pr; (2) = a plait; (3) = a plait made with 3 prs of passives; (4) = a double plait. The arrows indicate the direction of working.

7. Leaving out prs from the 1/2 st. block and adding in more prs if necessary, start at Z and work the first block tally. Try very hard to fill the square, keep the sides straight and make the tally nice and firm; in many examples of this type of lace the tallies are loose and only have a few rows of weaving, which quickly becomes untidy with use.

77

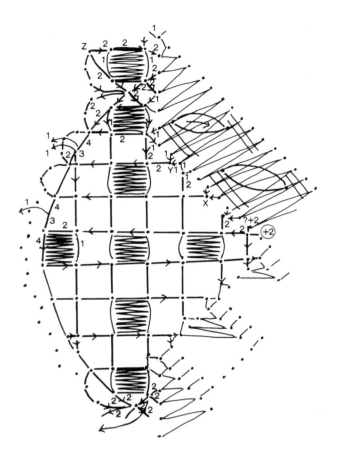

Fig. 7.3 The headside portion of 'Hettie'

Following the working diagram, and noting the following points, complete the headside fan:

(i) One pr of twisted threads lies down the side of every tally.

(ii) Make sure that your plaits are the correct length—remember Pat's rule (work your plait the length you think it should be then undo one stitch); it nearly always works, but be sure to check again, nevertheless.

(iii) The heading consists of a simple plaited loop with picots. In this pattern the picots are single as a coarse thread is being used.

(iv) Where prs come from the 1/2 st. block to work, and later go back into the block, they come as single twisted prs, being joined at Y, X, etc. with (1/2 st.; pin; 1/2 st.), and continuing as a plait.

(v) 3 prs are left out in the outer curved plaits of the fan and one in a plait at the tail end of the fan.

The footside and ground

8. These should present no problems. I used a twisted foot with 3 prs of passives, but the original had 2 prs of passives, and you may prefer this. The same message applies to the diagonal plaits as in note 2 above. As these plaits come and go into the footside at the same point you can try a slight variation (which could perhaps be called the 'traditional' way) of making a V-join. Using the footside workers, work wh. st. through the 2 prs of the plait. Put up a pin to the right of 2 prs, the workers and the l.h. plait pr; cover the pin with the 2 plait prs, i.e. the 2 r.h. prs, thus making the original workers one of the 'new' plait prs and the l.h. pr from the 'in' plait the new workers for the footside. This is only a slight variation from the way we usually work the join, but it does slightly affect the appearance of the join. As usual, having

tried both methods you can decide which way you prefer; my preference will be obvious, as I like to continue the appearance of the snatch pin loop. The links with the wh. and 1/2 st. blocks will be worked in the same way as described in note 4 above.

Work as much lace as you wish for the finished article, whether it is for trimming for a curtain, a holland blind or, as in the original, for a bed-valance or linen towels, and then finish off as appropriate.

Have fun! At first appearance this looks a formidable piece of lace, but being coarser than most patterns we are working in this book, once you have got the hang of the pattern it provides a welcome change and it actually grows quite quickly!

Lizzie

This is an old English Bedfordshire pattern, easily recognised by the square plaits (tallies). It probably dates from Victorian times, either late nineteenth century or early twentieth, and is typical of the patterns used by the old lacemakers when lacemaking was a cottage industry. It was given to Margaret Hamer by a descendant of one of these people, and I am grateful for her permission to use it. The bobble tallies appear in the centre of circular buds and in the sample (Plate 20) have been made slightly larger than is customary to show up clearly.

Materials: 22 prs of bobbins wound in No. 100 linen lace thread, with 8 additional prs for the corner; 1 large pin or *very* fine cocktail stick or toothpick.

To Work
You should have no problems in setting up, for this is really a very straightforward pattern, and if you have worked consistently through the book the only technique needing explanation is the bobble tally. Try to start at the base of the trail (marked X on the working diagram, Fig. 7.4) for this does give a much better finish. The footside can be worked either plain or twisted.

1. Work the trail, headside, footside, linking plaits and bud until you reach the centre of the bud where you should have a dot with a circle around it; this indicates a raised bobble tally, but beware! On many old patterns you will only find a single dot (or pin hole) in the centre of the bud.

To work a raised tally (Fig. 7.5)
2. The tally can be worked on either the right side of the work or the wrong side, remembering that the right side is underneath. If you work the bobble underneath the work it makes the final join much easier and it is better to use this method if you are working a round, square, oval or rectangular piece of lace. If you are working a straight strip, though, you will probably find your results, particularly the early ones, are better if the tallies are worked on top. To start with we will work the tally on top of the work.

3. Leaving the workers to the side (if following the drawn lines on Fig. 7.5 it will be to the left), find the 2 centre prs, work a half stitch with them, then put up a pin between them. Work a long straight plait (tally); the length of the plait (tally) will be a matter for your own personal decision and will depend partly on which stick you use to wrap the plait (tally) around—with a very fine toothpick for the base I worked a plait 6 mm long (25 complete turns) in this pattern but, as I already said, it is larger than I would normally make it.

4. When you are quite satisfied with both the appearance and the length of the plait, finish it off by putting bobbin no. 4 over no. 3, thus changing the position of these two threads. Lay the stick over the tally and twist the 2 prs of threads over the stick, down behind it, and out in front of the stick, as in Fig. 7.5c(i), so that the two prs of bobbins lie away from each other. Very carefully roll the stick up to the pin. Remove the pin from its original position and replace it under

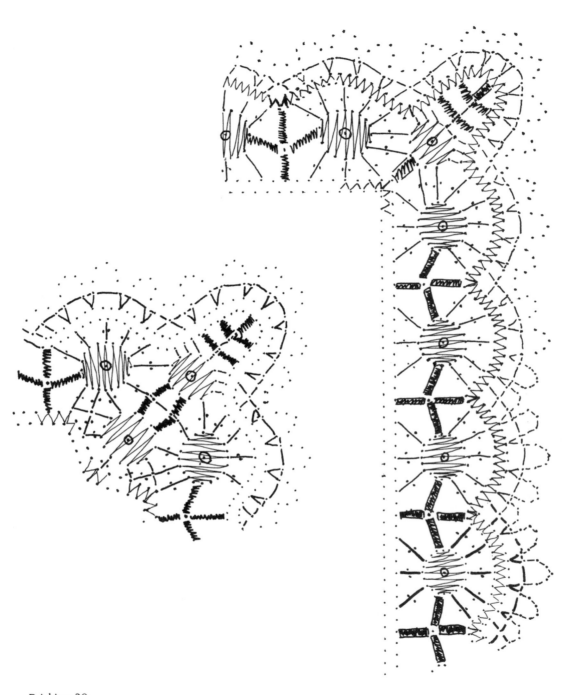

Pricking 20

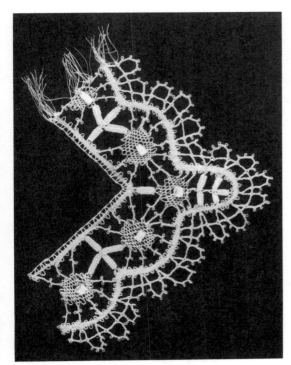

Plate 20 'Lizzie'—the simple corner

the stick, leaving the stick in place for the present—you will need to tuck it between 2 pins on each side. Work a half stitch with the 2 prs which worked the tally, find the original workers, and continue with the half stitch weaving, bringing the 2 prs from the tally back into the work. Complete the bud.

5. Work up to the corner, noting: (a) at the V-base of the trail you need to use a pin twice, therefore put up a pin the first time you meet the pin hole; gain on a pin the second time the pin needs to be used, and use the pin a second time for the final meeting; (b) great care needs to be taken in the centre of the 4 long plaits (tallies); it is not easy to keep the plaits straight in the centre; one tip is to ensure that the plaits are not too long.

The corner

6. You will need to add in 2 prs at the lower edge of the previous bud as indicated on the working diagram, Fig. 7.4.

7. The footside. Work up to the corner line, leaving out 2 prs on the inner side of the footside for the tally and gaining on a pin. The 2 prs can be left out *after* the pin, or one can be left out after pin

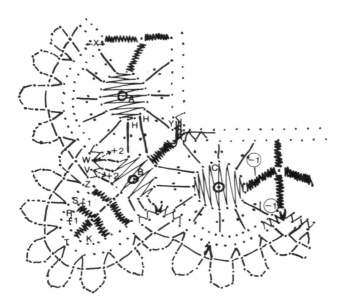

Fig. 7.4 Working diagram for the corner of 'Lizzie'

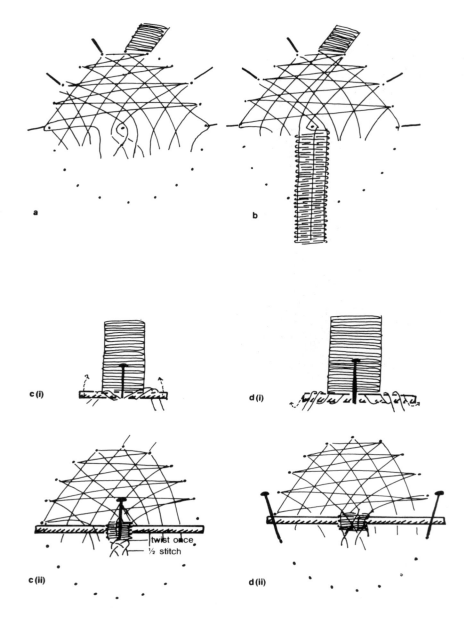

Fig. 7.5 Working a raised tally: **a** preparing to work the tally; **b** the tally worked, preparatory to rolling it up; **c(i)** rolling the tally on top of the work; **c(ii)** the completed tally; **d(i)** rolling the tally under the work; **d(ii)** the tally under the bud

Y and one after the corner pin, as in Fig. 7.6; the latter method gives a squarer start, but the pr on the left will need one twist before starting the tally. On the actual footside you will only need 1 twist where the pin holes are closer at the corner.

8. Work the headside and trail up to point z, adding in 2 prs each at W and V.

9. Work the plait (tally) from the corner point to bud B.

10. You are now ready to work the bud. Note that it is slightly smaller than those in the straight part

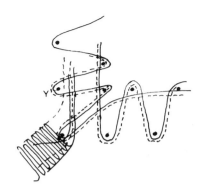

Fig. 7.6 The alternative ways of working the corner shown by: a continuous line; b broken line

of the pattern, so you will have to adjust the positioning of the prs used to work the bobble tally.

11. Work the headside trail up to T adding in one pr at each of the 2 adjoining pin holes S and R, and you are now ready to work firstly the 2 plaits (tallies) which run from the trail to the centre line, and then the line of 4 legs (plaits) which run from the bud B to the plait (tally) K. These legs run across the base of the first 2 plaits, picking up the r.h. pr from tallies (do *not* include the weavers of the tally), so that the legs (plaits) here are worked with 3 prs, each using (2 single threads, and 2 threads worked as one), taking the threads from l. to r. (l; l; ll; ll). Work the plait (tally) K.

12. Complete the headside trail and heading to the end of the corner, bringing in prs from the 3 plaits (tallies), and from the 3 legs from bud B to the trail, and leaving out 4 prs at appropriate places in the trail.

13. After working bud C you will have 2 extra prs, so take these out in the leg (plait) and plait (tally) as indicated on the working diagram, Fig. 7.4.

This 'straight' corner was adapted from the original shaped corner, which is given here, to be worked when these corners are reached. At this stage you are strongly advised to work the straight corner.

8 Fillings and grounds

So far we have looked at—and hopefully learnt—the basic techniques of the three laces in this family; we have, as it were, baked a cake. Now we are going to add the icing and the filling, by looking at some of the additional techniques which make the laces more interesting, both to work and to look at.

In this chapter we will learn some of the fillings and grounds which have been used in the past, but which do not occur very often in modern designs, with the exception of the first two fillings, point ground and honeycomb. I should point out that the fillings occur most frequently in laces of the Bedfordshire-Maltese variety. Maltese laces use a variety of the simpler grounds, in particular a version of the diamond filling or ground and one which is virtually exclusive to the Maltese lace, the so-called 'English ground'. Cluny lace uses the tulle (point ground) filling, but not much

else; these latter two laces tend to concentrate almost exclusively on design and the careful use of basic techniques to achieve their beauty and effect.

Many of the fillings and grounds have been borrowed from point ground lace, as might be expected when we remember that many of the Bedfordshire lacemakers turned originally from point ground lace to the Maltese style of lacemaking (see Introduction). Other fillings are taken from Honiton lace, here often being used as a ground rather than a filling. The best way to discover these fillings is to look at pieces of old lace, but unfortunately most of us do not have access to many of these, so books and photographs have to suffice. Do take advantage of looking at any old lace of this family that you can, and at any books which may have a bearing on this chapter.

Hedgehog

This pattern introduces the point ground filling, a simple ground—flower-centred braid—and a very simple heading—the twist and picot heading. You will notice that each of the three patterns in this chapter uses an oval shape to outline the fillings, although these are identical neither in shape nor in method of working. I have used this

outline for the fillings, as they are the purpose of these exercises, but hopefully you will also find the patterns a joy to work, and will want to make lengths suitable for use. The oval shape gives greater practice at fitting a filling into an outline than many other shapes do.

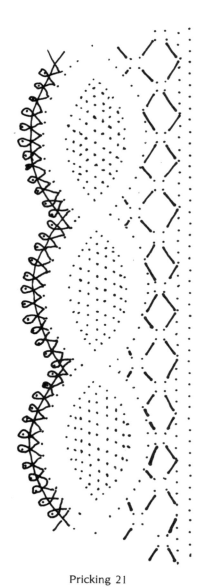

Pricking 21

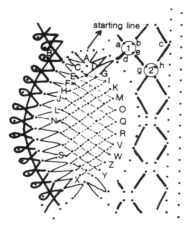

Plate 21 The filling: 'Hedgehog'

Fig. 8.1 Working diagram of the pattern 'Hedgehog'

Materials: 28 prs of bobbins wound in No. 80 linen lace thread or Bouc cotton No. 30/3.

To Work

Referring to working diagram, Fig. 8.1, start at the crossover between the two trails, making 3–4 additional pin holes, and hanging 16 prs evenly from the 5–6 pin holes. Leaving 3 prs passives plus 1 pr workers on the l.h. side, and 1 pr + 1 pr workers on the r.h. side, work the second part of a multi-crossing, i.e. cross 5 prs. Now work part

3 of the crossing, bringing the workers from each side through their respective prs to join with a (wh. st.; twist × 2; pin; wh. st.) at the central pin A.

The footside and ground

1. As no prs are carried through the footside in this pattern, a twisted footside is very appropriate here. The ground is flower-centred braid. Commencing at (a), (b) and (c), hang 2 prs from each pin. Starting at (b) weave a small square bud in wh. st., bringing in the 2 prs at (d) (Fig. 8.1) and

the final 2 prs at (e). Work plaits from (d) and (e), the prs from (d) going into the trail, and the plait from (e) being the l.h. pr for bud 2. This is worked similarly, using these 2 prs to go into the bud at (g), and the 2 prs hung on pin (c) to work the plait, those 2 prs start the bud at (h).

Note: When putting up a pin, twist the workers once to make a strong edge, and twist all 4 prs once before going into the final plaits.

The trails
2. Now start on the outer trail and heading, working the basic trail with 5 prs of constant passives, and the heading with 2 prs which are hung from pin B. The trail is whole stitch.

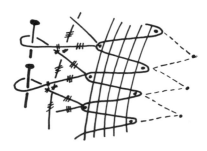

Fig. 8.2   The heading

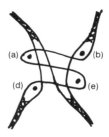

Fig. 8.3   The 'flower centre' of the ground

The heading (Fig. 8.2)
3. The heading is a simple twist and picot heading; this does not occur very frequently but is a quick, easy and narrow heading, and it makes a pleasing alternative to the more usual 9-pin or Cluny heads.

Linking at every pin, except for the one at the base of the V, the heading is worked with 2 prs of twisted threads, so hang them from pin B. (Twist each pr 3 times and link the r.h. pr into the trail. Twist this pr × 3; cross the 2 prs with a (wh. st.; twist each pr × 2). Work a single picot; twist × 2, giving 1 extra twist to the l.h. pr; wh. st.; tw. × 3.)

The filling
4. Using the pairs from C and D which have been left out from the trail, twist each pr 2–3 times. Those who are familiar with point ground will be used to twisting each pr twice, but here it is sometimes necessary to give a third twist to adequately cover the distance between two pin holes. Work (half st.; twist × 2; pin; *do not cover*). The l.h. pr will link with the trail at E, being picked up by the workers, and coming straight out again. Now we can start to get into a pattern of work; starting at the r.h. pr from the pin G, work a similar stitch at the next diagonal pin hole, with the pr from E, and finally in this row a third pin using the l.h. pr from the last hole, and the pr which was left out of the trail at F. This row is linked into the outer trail at H.

5. This pattern of work is continued throughout the filling, as you will see from the working diagram, Fig. 8.1; towards the end of the filling, pairs will come into the trail, and stay there, to be left out when appropriate.

This filling should cause you no difficulty, as long as you stick to the main rule of *always* working in straight rows, starting at the top of a block of filling and working right down the row. You are not bound to start at the right hand side—the left may seem happier to you—but whichever way you choose to work, you *must* keep to it if you do not wish to get into a complete mess.

Having completed the filling you may need to fill in some of the ground, then return to the trails and work your multi-crossing.

Repeat the pattern as often as desired, and really enjoy it!

Connie

Pricking 22

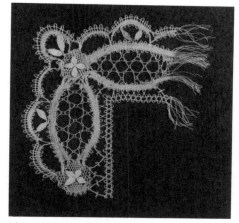

Plate 22   The filling: 'Connie'

This pattern introduces the second most widely used filling in Bedfordshire-Maltese lace, the honeycomb filling. We also used raised tallies in a modified way, by taking pairs from the bud to work two tallies, crossing them in the centre and then working a further two tallies, giving the appearance of a raised flower.

Materials: Appoximately 30 prs of bobbins as indicated on the working diagram, Fig. 8.4. Note the large number of prs needed for the half stitch bud, owing to the 4 prs to be taken out for the raised tallies; it is very important that allowance is made for such tallies when setting up (or by adding in extra prs) to avoid having a very starved bud after taking out prs for the tallies.

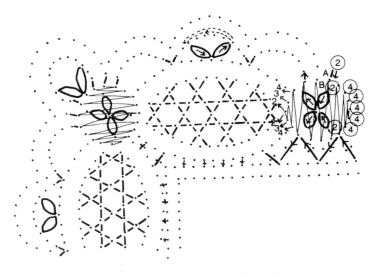

Fig. 8.4 Working diagram for the start of 'Connie'

Neither the headside nor the footside should present any problems so they will be omitted from the discussion here, but do watch for the 4 kisses linking the footside with the inner trail; if you have problems with the corner, refer back to the pattern 'Glifada', page 37.

The bud

1. Work up to B, remembering to bring in 2 prs at A which in later repeats will come from the headside; it is so easy to overlook these prs when setting up that constant reminders are worthwhile!

Check very carefully that you have the correct row before starting the raised tallies, which are worked exactly as a single one. When you reach the join in the centre of the 4 tallies, check carefully that the tallies are the exact length, then cross them with a windmill crossing. They are *not* linked with the bud at this stage.

Work the third and fourth tallies, covering them, as in the pattern 'Hettie', then work the bud to the point where the prs from the tallies come back into it. Bring them in to the bud again, checking carefully to ensure that you have the best point for doing so, then complete the bud.

The link between the oval trails and the bud

2. As in 'Georgina' you may like—as I do—to make a clear distinction between the two features; I feel

that there are too many prs to just twist them, so divide the threads into groups and work short plaits with them.

The oval trails and filling

3. Work the l.h. trail to C and the r.h. trail to D, following the working diagram, Fig. 8.5. Leave out a single pr at each of the points indicated on the pricking and diagram, except at pin D where a pr joins the trail from the filling and goes straight out again. Twist the prs from H and F twice; at G work a honeycomb stitch, i.e. (half stitch; twist × 1; pin; half st.; twist × 1). These 2 prs then deviate—the l.h. pr goes to the left where a

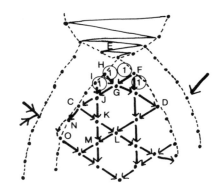

Fig. 8.5 The start of the honeycomb filling

honeycomb stitch is worked with the pr (twisted) from I; the l.h. pr from G then goes to J where it meets a 'new' pr from the trail, coming out directly again to meet with the r.h. pr at K; honeycomb stitch; r.h. pr to L; l.h. pr to M, etc. Go back to C where, in addition to the linking pr coming out of the trail, a second pr is brought out and twisted to cover the side of the honeycomb hole from C to N, where it goes back into the trail, to come out again at O. Leave the l.h. side temporarily and work up to L on the r.h. side where the 2 sides join.

Written like this it all seems very complicated, but you will find it really easy to work if you just carefully watch the shape of the 6-sided honeycomb holes and make sure that you follow the links exactly as given in the working diagram. Remember that in the first half of the filling all prs either come out and stay out of the trails to work the filling or link back in, to come directly out again; in the second half all prs come back into the trails, either to remain in the trail or to link in and out. Less commonly, though, a pair will come into the trail, stay in for one hole then come out again. This happens at O in this pattern, and is merely a variant of the direct in-out link.

The corner (Fig. 8.6)
4. This is quite straightforward once you have decided where to start and how many additional

pairs you need to work it. In this instance the work has been done for you, *if* you choose to follow the suggestions I have made! As usual, before starting to work the corner take a good look at it, and with a pencil trace the lines of the workers for the bud, if possible without looking at the working diagram. You would expect to start the bud, as you do in the majority of buds, where the two main trails come into it. However, on tracing the lines of the workers for this corner bud you will discover that this would land you with all your pairs coming into the heading at the end. It is thus necessary to try another starting point, so look for a point where several pairs come into the bud from other parts of the pattern. Yes, the first place to try would be the point where three plaits (in this pattern, normally at least two prs, from plaits or tallies) link into the bud at adjoining pin holes. Trace the lines of your workers from here, taking the point where the central plait comes in as your starting point. Where does this land you? Yes, you're correct—right where you want it, at the start of the two trails immediatley after the corner. Finally, you will need to ask yourself if the number of pairs you will have in the bud is adequate; to a certain extent you will not know this until you start to work, so always have extra pairs wound and available for a corner. In this pattern you will find that you need quite a few extra pairs—9 in all—to give a firm bud, and to ensure that you have sufficient prs to work all the plaits, tallies, etc. which are involved.

5. To work the bud, start at A, and work in half stitch as far as C, noticing especially that the two pairs from the l.h. plait are needed to work the headside trail, so 2 prs must be added in to compensate for these in the bud. You will also need additional prs at the start to give enough for the bud and to leave out the prs for the flower tallies, so add in 3 extra prs at pin B and a further 2 prs at pin C—you will have taken out the prs to work the first tally of the flower before prs are brought in from the outer trail to compensate for them. 4 prs come into the bud from each of the pins at the end of the outer trail, and 4,3,4 respectively from the pins of the inner trail. Turning to the l.h. side, the two tallies inside the curve of the heading follow the usual pattern; the first tally goes out to the heading, and the second

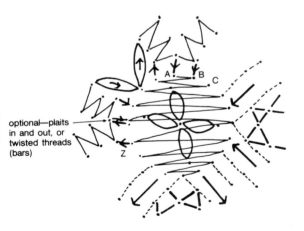

optional—plaits in and out, or twisted threads (bars)

Fig. 8.6 The corner bud

returns, so to avoid starving the buds at this point 2 more prs will probably need to be added in. Work the corner scallop in its entirety, bringing in the inner r.h. pr(s) to the bud, and taking out the l.h. pr(s.

6. Finally, before completing the bud, you have to decide where you will leave out the additional pairs that you added in to work it. Following Fig. 8.6, leave out 4 prs for plait Z, then, working a double plait, you can probably 'lose' two prs while working the plait. Start the headside trail with 2 extra prs of bobbins in it, and lose these at suitable places on the first few rows. At the conclusion of the bud you will probably have 22 prs to be divided between the two main trails; leave out the prs as indicated on the working diagram, and then lose 2 prs from each trail during the first few rows of working. Remember, once again, that the number of pairs that I quote is only a guide, and you may have more or less; don't worry about this as long as *you* are satisfied with the end result.

Fillings sampler—Spring

While I prefer to make lace which can be used, rather than samplers, there are times when the latter are of great value, both as learning devices and later as tools of reference. How often in lacemaking do we use our 'favourite' filling when there are many others which might give a more interesting, better balanced result. Only by having the actual fillings in front of you can you see at a single glance what the options are, and be reminded of all the choices.

The main sampler, however, is designed to be used as a piece of lace, too, probably using just one or two fillings. For the sake of space here I have not repeated the point ground or honeycomb fillings, but to provide a true record they should be included in either the 'Spring' sampler or in the additional blocks of fillings. I do not pretend that this selection of fillings is complete; apple blossom and mayflower both have alternative versions which I have only mentioned, and one or two other grounds will be included in later patterns.

Materials: 38–40 prs of bobbins wound in Molnylycke cotton quilting thread, approximately equivalent to No. 70–80 DMC Cordonnet. If this thread is difficult to obtain, the Mettler equivalent (40/3) is ideal. Alternatively you can use any of the equivalent threads listed in Appendix 1.

To Work
(Fig. 8.7) Before starting the first filling you may find it helpful to mark in the full honeycomb filling as in Fig. 8.4 and 8.5 ('Connie'), so that you can see where the whole stitch buds, called 'mayflowers', lie, and where the individual honeycombs share sides and pin holes with the mayflower buds. In future you probably will not have a working diagram to help you with this, so it is a good idea to get used to marking it in until you are quite familiar with the method of working.

Now let's get going! We will start with the footside ground tallies and crossed plaits. This portion of the pattern should present no difficulties if you note the following points:

1. The footside has a snatch pin edge; the 2 prs of passives on each side are worked as a normal twisted footside, and they are linked at every alternate hole with (tw. × 3 on each side; wh. st.; tw. × 2; pin; tw. × 3) (Fig. 8.7a).

2. In the ground most of the crossings are windmills, but there is one 6-point crossing at X (Fig. 8.7b).

3. A few of the tallies work in a reverse direction to the norm, e.g. you would expect tally Y to be worked from the footside to the trail, but in fact it is worked in the reverse direction; similarly on the other side (Fig. 8.7b) tally Z is worked in the

Pricking 23

Plate 23   The sampler 'Spring'

reverse direction. These tallies need careful working, and it is best to push down all pins around the tally and to give your pillow a quarter turn so that you are working the tally towards you, as is usual.

4. When crossing the trails in a multi-crossing, if all the pairs are used as in the first crossing above, the crossing tends to be very bulky and it is difficult to pull it up so that it lies flat. The appearance of the crossing can be greatly improved by carrying around 2 prs on each side and just crossing 4 prs.

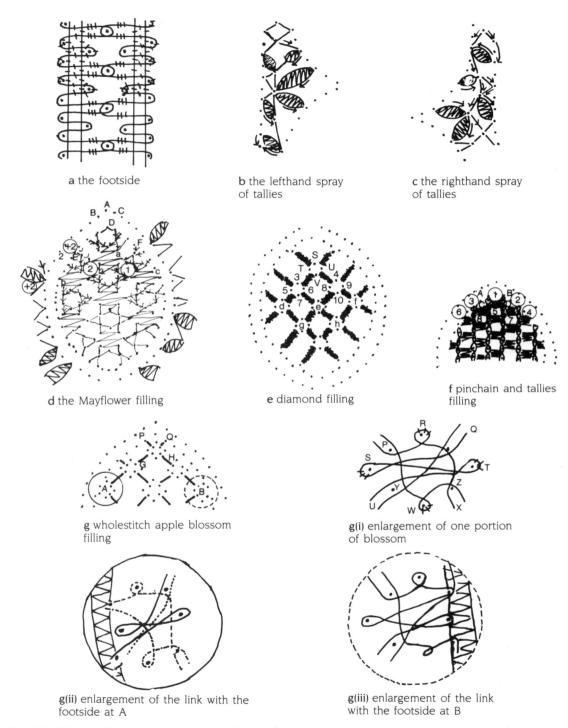

a the footside

b the lefthand spray of tallies

c the righthand spray of tallies

d the Mayflower filling

e diamond filling

f pinchain and tallies filling

g wholestitch apple blossom filling

g(i) enlargement of one portion of blossom

g(ii) enlargement of the link with the footside at A

g(iii) enlargement of the link with the footside at B

Fig. 8.7 Working diagrams of portions of the sampler of fillings
NB: In g(ii) and g(iii), the footside pin holes are not meant to be accurate, but merely indicate the position of the footside

The trails and first filling—Mayflower

1. Looking at Fig. 8.7d, hang 14 prs on pin A and work a multi-crossing, working 7 prs through 7 prs and bringing the outer prs from B and C back through their prs to meet at D.

2. Start on the r.h. trail and work to E, leaving out 1 pr at each inner pin; work the l.h. trail to F similarly. Starting at G work the first mayflower, in wh. st. with 1 twist at each pin. This bud fills a honeycomb hole, extending in the centre to an extra pin hole on each side—as can be clearly seen in Fig. 8.7d. Bring in one pr at each pin as the bud gets wider, and leave out 1 pr as it gets narrower.

3. Work the honeycomb holes 1 and 2 as far as you can, noting that the top r.h. hole on the l.h. honeycomb, and the top l.h. hole on the r.h. honeycomb, have already been worked as part of the mayflower bud, and the lower l.h. pr and lower r.h. pr will be parts of the mayflower buds (b) and (c). Mayflower bud (c) links 3 pins with the trail; workers meet at each of the points where the trail and bud adjoin.

Continue working in this way until you reach the widest point of the filling, then you will find that you will have to start transferring prs from the filling to the trail.

Diamond filling

1. The second filling used here is the diamond filling or ground (Fig. 8.7e). The version used here is borrowed from Devonshire (Honiton) lace. An alternative version occurs in Maltese lace and you will meet it in the collar in Chapter 10.

Two pairs are used for each tally (plait), which can either be taken out from the edging at a single point or, as in this case, 1 pr is taken out at each of two adjoining pins, and before starting out to work each tally you link them together with a (half st.; pin; half st.) using the single hole between the trail and the start of the tally.

To work the filling

2. Start the tallies as described above. *Work square-ended tallies until you reach the pins ST and SU; twist each pr 2–3 times (making sure that the centre does not look too bulky), then put up pins between the 2 prs at ST and the 2 prs at SU; give 3 twists to each pr after the pins. Take the 2 centre prs and cross them with a (wh. st.; twist × 2–3); *no pin*. Work (wh. st.; pin; tw. × 2–3) with each of the 2 side prs, then (wh. st.; tw. × 2–3; *no pin*); with the centre prs.**

Work tallies 3 and 4, thus completing 1 diamond. Next, the diamonds made up of tallies 3,5,6 and 7; and 4,8,9 and 10, are worked as from * to ** above.

3. The first half is completed by working the row of three diamonds below this one; none of these should cause you any problems, except, perhaps, in getting and keeping the tallies even, both in size and length! In the row below, i.e. that which completes the diamonds (d), (e) and (f) and starts tallies (g) and (h), care must be taken where the filling adjoins the trail.

Pin chain and tallies filling

1. Once again, have a good look at the pricking before rushing in to start—always a great temptation! Here, in Fig. 8.7f, you see single rows of pin holes, indicating a pin chain, linked by tallies. Notice, too, that the tallies occupy a small rectangular block, i.e. they lie between 4 pin holes; there is another filling occasionally used in Bedfordshire lace where the tallies just link 2 opposite pins, as in the cucumber foot, so be careful not to confuse the two.

Pin chain is just an ongoing row of honeycomb stitches, i.e. (half st.; twist; pin; half st.; twist pin; half st.; twist pin, etc.).

The pin chain and tallies filling is thus worked: starting with the 4 central prs, 2 coming out of the r.h. side trail and 2 from the l.h. side trail, work 1 hole of pin chain (as above) on each side. Using the central pr from each of these pin chain holes work a tally to exactly fit the space between A,B,C and D of Fig. 8.7f; the other pr on each side will have 2 twists already so no more will be needed before finishing off the tally with pin chain holes in C and D, remembering to finish off (and work the next tally) on the right before working the l.h. side in order to stabilise the tally; if you are accustomed to taking the worker on one position, thus leaving it in the 3rd position, you will finish off on the left hand side first. Continue the filling, bringing in prs from the trail where necessary, and working the tallies in numerical order, continuing in the same pattern after the numbers run out on the diagram.

Whole stitch apple blossom filling (Figs. 8.7g and g(i)).

1. Work plaits from the two trails starting at P and Q; pin between each of these prs. Take the l.h. pr from P and work wh. st. through r.h. pr from P. Twist × 3; double right-handed picot at R, work wh. st. through prs from Q. Leave this pr.

2. Take the r.h. pr from Q (now 2nd from r.) and wk. wh. st. to the left through 2 prs; picot and pin in S.

3. Wh. st. through 3 prs to the right; tw. × 3; picot and pin in T.

4. Wh. st. through 3 prs to the left; pin in Y and leave.

5. Take to the right the last pr that you have just passed through; wk. 1 wh. st. to the right; double left-handed picot in W; wh. st. through the last pr to the right and leave; this pr will become the 1st pr for the plait U, the second pr being the last pr of passives.

6. Work plaits U and X to pins G and H.

There are two places where the link between the filling and the trail is not quite so simple, as you do not have an entire filling. The answer is to work the 'blossom' so that it is as nearly complete as possible, using all the pin holes that you are given, but without adding any! One way of dealing with this little problem is shown in Figs. 8.7g(ii) and (iii).

Further fillings

Cord filling or ground. This is not used very often, but when it does occur it is an interesting variation, with attractive crossings of the 4 twisted bars. Follow Figs. 8.8 and 8.9 while working.

1. Start by linking in 2 prs at each of 2 adjoining pin holes, or in this case, a pure sampler, hang them from the top two adjoining pin holes.

2. Twist each pr twice.

3. Put a pin between the 2 r.h. prs; work a wh. st. with these 2 prs.

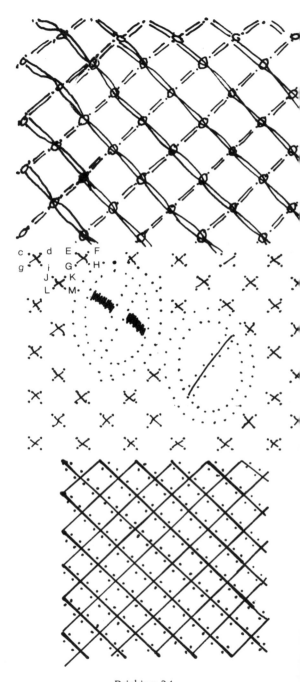

Pricking 24

Plate 24 Further fillings: from the top,
cord filling; two ovals with trail and tallies
in the upper and feather bar in the lower,
and a background of feather filling.

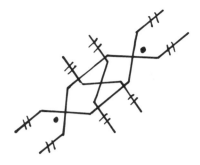

Fig. 8.8 Cord ground filling

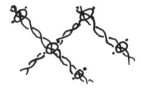

Fig. 8.9 Starting a block in cord ground

Fig. 8.10 Cord ground as a filling; note the twists

4. Take the 2 l.h. prs and work a wh. st. through
the r.h. pr.

5. Work a wh. st. with these 2 l.h. prs, then a
further wh. st. through the 2 r.h. prs. Twist the
original l.h. prs (now lying to the right of the 4
prs) twice.

6. Work a wh. st. with the 2 original prs (now lying
to the left of the 4 prs). Put a pin between these
2 prs then twist each pr twice.

Continue with the pattern as given above, working
in diagonal rows either from left to right or from
right to left, filling in any space at the end of the
block of filling with half rows if necessary.

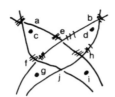

Fig. 8.11 Four-pin filling

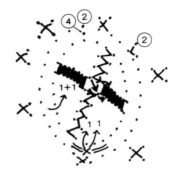

Fig. 8.12 Snatch pin bars with tallies filling

Four pin filling

This is another ground borrowed from Honiton lace (Fig. 8.11). The pricking shows a 'box' of four holes, and in a block these boxes alternate in consecutive rows. To work the filling:

1. Following Fig. 8.11, twist the 2 prs on A × 3—these are either new prs or they can come from the filling as in this case. Wh. st. with these 2 prs; pin.

2. Tw. the 2 prs at B × 3; wh. st. with these 2 prs; pin.

3. Tw. the 2 centre prs × 3; wh. st.; *no pin.***

4. Tw. the 2 l.h. prs × 3; wh. st.; pin; tw. × 3.

5. Tw. the 2 l.h. prs × 3; wh. st.; pin; tw. × 3.

6. Wh. st. with centre prs; *no pin*; tw. × 3.

Start at the top again and repeat from * to ** for boxes E, F, G and H, then for J, K, L and M, working the latter with the 2 prs from i and the 2 prs from G. Finally in this portion of ground—in this pattern—work the 4th group of pin holes.

7. Work the 12 half-groups of 4 pins on the r.h. side of the top oval, starting with the 5 groups along the top edge, but working on the diagonal as soon as possible.

Snatch pin bars with tallies filling

1. This filling tends to occur singly within a circle or an oval, although this is by no means exclusive, hence I have put it in an oval framework. This is worked similarly to the outline trails in 'Helianthus' (Chapter 3). Start by laying in 4 prs of passives (or 6 if preferred), and hanging on 2 prs for the workers. Work until you reach the start of the snatch pin trail and the square-ended tally. 2 prs of passives leave the trail at a single point, and at the next following pin the workers leave

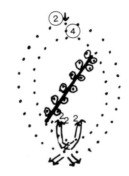

Fig. 8.13 Feather filling

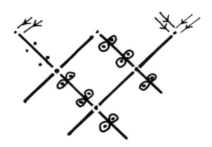

Fig. 8.14 Feather ground

the oval trail. The square-ended tally also is worked with 2 prs left out at successive holes; it crosses the snatch pin trail the Cluny way and the prs rejoin the trail on the opposite side at successive pins.

2. While working the lower half of the r.h. trail leave out 2 prs (at different spots), which will leave you with 2 prs on each side of the lower point

of the oval; throw out 1 pr on each side, and knot (with a reef knot) the remaining 2 × 1 threads, sewing the ends back into your work, or just cutting off close to the work.

3. The second oval has a single line of feather filling (Fig. 8.13). Start as for the first oval and work until you reach the plait with tallies on either side. 2 prs for the plait are left out at a single pin hole, and the diagonal bar is merely a plait with tallies on either side; this simple filling can look very attractive providing the picots are well made, so do take care over these. In normal work the holes in the prickings, for both this filling and the previous one, and the cord and 4-pin grounds, are considerably closer together, so imagine all reduced by about half as they would appear in a regular pattern.

4. Complete the oval as for the first one.

While working these two ovals with their fillings you will have had to work small portions of the 4-pin ground to have prs in the correct place; now finish off the 4-pin filling, throwing out 1 pr at each of the edges on the last row, in preparation for working the final filling.

Feather ground (Fig. 8.14)

This filling really needs no description; it consists of two rows of plaits, one which is a straight plait, and one which has picots on both sides. Note, however, that these picots do not alternate as usual, but are directly opposite each other, so work them as follows: (picot on one side—say the r.h. side; wh. st. and twist with the central pr; picot on the l.h. side); finish off as usual with (tw.; wh. st.; tw.), then on into the plait. All crossings are windmills.

As I have already mentioned, there are quite a few other fillings which I have not the space to describe; many are simple to work, as the feather ground above, and therefore really do not need description; others are variants of those described above, such as the 6-pin mayflower; apple blossom, etc. They only occur very rarely in Bedfordshire-Maltese patterns, whereas those I have described above are found frequently in the old examples of this variety of lace, whenever fillings or grounds have been used.

9 More about footsides

So far in this book we have used a plain footside with a straight edge and one with a snatch pin edge; a twisted footside (in both a piece of lace and an insertion); a kat-stitch footside, a cucumber foot, and several variations of these basic feet. In this chapter we start by working a piece of lace with a waved footside, following it with a shaped corner, and finally one of the less usual footsides to which I have given the name 'crossroads foot' because of its similarity to the pattern of that name.

Mollie

This is the second piece of Spanish Cluny referred to in Chapter 7. It is a very simple but effective design, and results in a lace which is pleasing in appearance and quick to execute. The only intricate feature is the central crossing of the tallies which form the flower; I have never met a crossing exactly like this before, but by carefully undoing a crossing on the original piece of lace from which I drew the pattern, I was assured that I was correct in my magnifying glass reading. Try

Plate 25 'Mollie'

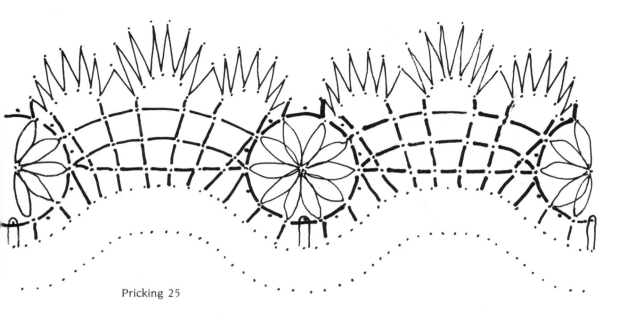

Pricking 25

this crossing, and see what you feel about it; if dissatisfied, try another one.

Materials: Approximately 27 prs of bobbins, wound in No. 50 linen lace thread, or the equivalent cotton thread.

To Work

Hang on 27 prs as indicated on the working diagram, Fig. 9.1.

Work the following features of the pattern in this order:

1. The lower 5 tallies of the flower. Take either the r.h. pr or the l.h. pr of the 10; work wh. st. through all the other prs; repeat with the second outside pr (r. or l.h. according to the one you used the first time); this is merely to support the prs and is a set-up procedure, not part of the normal crossing.

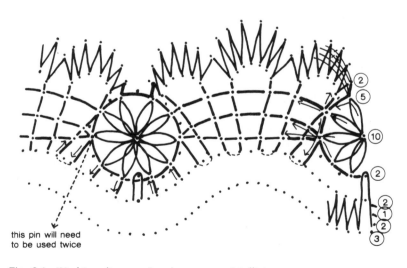

this pin will need to be used twice

Fig. 9.1 Working diagram for the pattern 'Mollie'

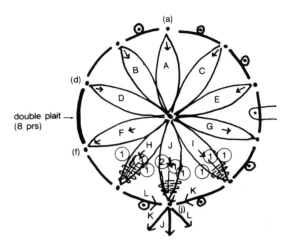

Fig. 9.2 Working diagram of the tallies and ring

Work the 5 petal-shaped tallies in the order shown on the working diagram, Fig. 9.2, i.e. 1-F, 2-G, 3-H, 4-I and finally J. The reason for the careful ordering is that with 10 tallies they inevitably lie partly on top of each other, and it looks much neater to have the flower petals well ordered.

2. Start the footside and plaited ring (around the flower); the method of working the footside is no different from that for a straight footside but great care needs to be taken with the 'waves' to keep the braid even. On the first row of the footside an extended loop is worked to join it with the initial ring pin; twist as many times as you think necessary to form a firm loop.

3. Start the headside, using as many prs of passives as you need to create the effect you want. This, of course, will mean adjusting the number of starting prs on the outermost pins. Work the first scallop—note that my scallops are linked by a short plait, but if you have adjusted the number of pairs in the heading you may need to adjust this too.

4. Finally, work the ring. In future repeats this will start at (a) and you work down each side, joining at the centre bottom (j); here at the start only half the circle is worked and the two plaits are worked down each side, with the usual link. Note the picots on the plaits which help to keep the ring in shape—and that I inadvertently

omitted a couple on the sample! (Plate 25); a double plait, i.e. work a plait using 4 × 2 threads, is worked from (d) to (f).

The pattern should present no further problems until you reach the central crossing of the flower. Work the 5 upper petals following the order shown on the working diagram, Fig. 9.1—i.e. a, b, c, etc.

5. Now refer to Fig. 9.3b; work a 6-plait crossing with the prs from A, B and C, putting up a pin in the centre as usual. Take the prs from E and pass one under all the prs from B, A and C, and one over all the pairs. Knot all the prs once. It is essential for a neat crossing that the crossing is eased up carefully and thoroughly after each move, and no matter how you normally start your tally, a stitch is vital after this crossing—I still prefer a half stitch, but you may find that a whole stitch holds the bobbins in place better to start with.

You should have no further difficulties with this pattern, but one final reminder—tension, and plaits which are neither too short nor too long, and a very neat, well spaced footside are the keys to a really good piece of lace. Just because this piece is simpler than some of those you have worked recently it is all too easy to rush the work and forget to pay attention to these vital points.

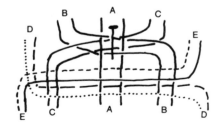

Fig. 9.3 The central crossing of the flowers: a crossing the outer pairs; b the full crossing

Further development

This pattern is one which lends itself to reduction; you can either redraw the pricking on to a smaller sized graph (the original was drawn on an 8 to 25 cm grid—although this has little relevance apart from keeping the drawing really accurate), or use a reducing photocopier, bearing in mind the points I have already raised about this means of reproduction.

Tassie

This pattern can only be called an 'amalgam of styles'. We have the Cluny divided trail, making the half-moon shape; a heading which is used in both Cluny and Bedfordshire laces; Bedfordshire apple blossom ground, and one version of the split trail, largely used in Bedfordshire-Maltese lace.

The pattern is dedicated to the Lacemakers of Tasmania, with whom I was spending a very happy ten days when I originally drew up this pattern.

Materials: 25–27 prs of bobbins wound in Mettler cotton quilting thread, No. 40/3. This cotton is currently (1990) widely available, in a variety of colours, from shops specialising in materials for quilting.

To Work

The pattern as given consists largely of the corner—for reasons of space—the actual pattern repeat being from A to B (Fig. 9.4).

1. Start at A with the footside—a plain one with a straight edge, having 2 prs of passives. Add in prs for the trail as indicated on the working diagram, Fig. 9.4, and work the divided trail up to C where 2 prs are added in. These are taken through the trail (see Chapter 5 if necessary), the first pr joining the original workers to work the plait from D to E which goes straight into a petal tally for the flower. This arrangement is frequently found in Bedfordshire lace, but this is the first time we have met it in these pages.

2. Continue the trail to F, then you will have to turn to the flower. Here we work a different arrangement of tallies in a 6-petalled flower: petals 1 and 2 work in to the centre and are crossed in a windmill crossing—see Fig. 9.5; the right 2 prs from the tally are 'left behind' and the left 2 prs go out in a tally. Later, a plait, followed by tally 4, comes from the garland, through the trail, and works the plait, then tally 4. Tallies 1 and 4 are crossed with a windmill crossing, taking out the central pin, then replacing it in its 'new' position, pulling the second crossing as firmly as possible. Tallies 5 and 6 are then worked outwards with these 4 prs to F, where they pass through the trail; and out in a small plait of the garland of leaves.

The garland

3. The garland is worked with 4 prs of bobbins, the pattern being worked as in Fig. 9.6; the prs from the tallies either stay in the trail for a short distance before going out again or are used to work a Cluny crossing (through the divided trail) in either direction.

Outer trail

4. The outer trail has pin holes directly opposite each other on the 2 sides, and this indicates a split trail, version A. There are 2 prs of constant passives and 1 pr of workers on each side; the workers go through the prs on their respective sides, cross in the centre with (tw.; wh. st.; tw.) and then continue on to work the edge pins. Cluny crossings are worked from C to D and G inwards, F to H and J outwards; K to L and M inwards; N and O to P outwards; and Q and R to S outwards. A second variation of the split trail occurs in the 'horseshoes' in the pattern 'Pam' in Chapter 11.

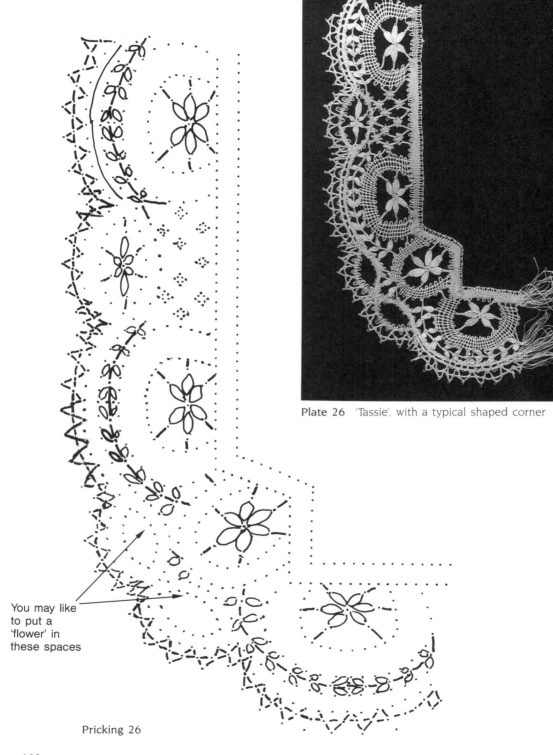

You may like
to put a
'flower' in
these spaces

Plate 26 'Tassie', with a typical shaped corner

Pricking 26

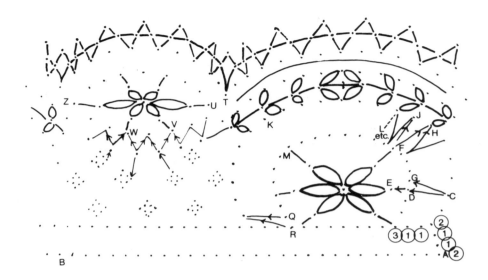

Fig. 9.4 Working diagram for the pattern 'Tassie'

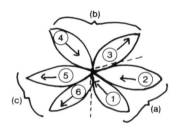

Fig. 9.5 Working order of the central flower

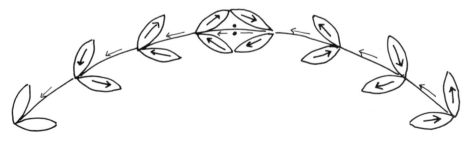

Fig. 9.6 The garland

The heading

5. The heading should present no problems; note that the central, gently curved pr links into the split trail at T.

The small oval

6. The small oval near the headside is worked with a plain trail, again having 2 prs of constant passives on each side of the central flower. The

103

outer flower is worked in the traditional manner with 3 prs coming in (2 prs being added in at U), a 6-plait crossing in the centre, and the same 3 prs going out.

The inner side (of the oval) uses Cluny crossings at V and W and 2 prs from the ground come into and out of the trail in the centre.

7. The multi-crossing at each end of the oval trails is slightly unusual. To work the crossing at the top of the oval the central pin is put up in the centre (crossing point) of the trail, and 2 prs + workers go to the r. of it, and 2 prs + workers go to the left of it; the workers cover the pin with (wh. st.; twist), each pr then going out to its respective side hole. The crossing is worked as usual with 2 prs on each side, then the workers are brought back to the lower central pin (wh. st.; twist; pin; wh. st.; twist). At the bottom of the oval the crossing is slightly more complicated; 2 prs are thrown out of the outer trail, leaving 2 prs + workers in the l.h. trail (including one pr from the lowest plait), and 2 prs + workers in the r.h. trail. Put up a pin at Z between the 2 prs of workers, with 1 pr from the lowest plait joining each side trail. Carry 2 prs around on the l.h. side, and work a multi-crossing with 2 prs on each side, but there is no 4th pin for this crossing. Take the pr left at (a) and work through all the prs to B. Work back to the left through 4 prs; leave. Take the next pr on the left of the l.h. trail (or the 9th pr from the right) and you are now ready to work the next portion of the split trail.

The corner (Fig. 9.8)

8. Turn to the half-moon (divided) trail. The 4 prs for the passives have been carried through the footside from the previous half-moon, and now come back into use. The rest of the pattern is basically the same as the main portion of the lace already worked; any slight changes should be quite apparent. Remember that this is worked Cluny fashion, with prs from the apple blossom ground, the garland tallies, etc. being carried through the trail and out into the central flower, or back to the garland, as the pattern dictates.

9. The garland is extended at the corner end, finally disappearing into the corner half-moon; 2 prs have to be left out near the start of the central

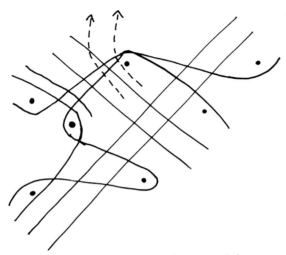

Fig. 9.7 Crossing the trails at the start of the corner

plait, and 2 prs need to be added in to work the penultimate central tally (see Fig. 9.8).

10. The split trail and heading need no explanation; leave out 2 prs from the trail at the first multi-crossing of the corner to reduce bulk, as they are no longer needed here.

11. The corner ovals each have 2 plaits and 1 tally leaving/joining them. The central crossing here, being longer than a multi-crossing, is worked as a continuation of the weaving (see Fig. 9.8). The final crossing of the corner is a basic multi-crossing.

12. The half-moon trail should present no difficulties; the 2 prs brought into it from the central plait of the garland are left out, after being briefly worked into the trail for security. 2 prs are added in at pin z to link the 2 adjoining half-moon trails, and one for the garland plait.

The footside

13. In all corners there has to be considerable multi-use of the corner pins; my preference is to use the pin twice only, and if more use of it is needed, to gain on pins between, as in Fig. 9.8. For the first sharp corner at v I used the pin; gained on a pin × 3; and finally used the inner central pin a second time. The central 'bend', running in to the mounting, is not so sharp so

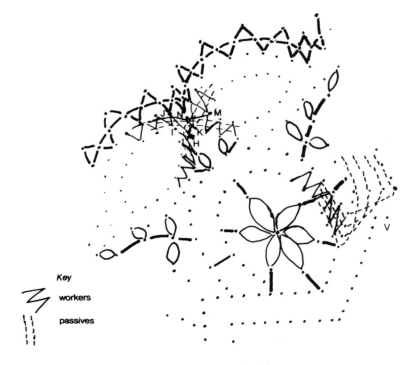

Fig. 9.8 Working diagram of the corner

I worked (pin; gain × 2; pin) and the final inner 'corner' is also (pin; gain × 2; pin). 2 prs are left out between corners 2 and 3.

As the rest of the pattern is a repeat of that worked already you should now be able to romp ahead!

Possible uses for this piece of lace are to edge the yoke of a dress or nightdress, to put on the front of a sachet, or—as it is fairly substantial—it is suitable for any oblong or square piece of domestic linen.

The alternative corner for 'Lizzie', Chapter 7
Now that you have worked a shaped corner, you might like to re-work 'Lizzie'—or at least to work a sample of it for your reference book, using the original corner.

Bicentenary

This piece of lace was designed to celebrate Australia's bicentenary in 1988, and is allegorical in design. Very obviously, we have the boomerang, known the world over as a weapon originally used by the Aborigines, the first and native people of the great island continent of Australia, when they had to kill the native animals for food. The cross of four tallies represents not only Christians, but people of all faiths who have since 1788 settled in Australia, whether as forced (i.e. convicts) or free men. The dove carrying the olive branch represents the peace and harmony between the two groups of Australian peoples for which now, after almost 200 years of repression of the Aborigines, we are hopefully striving. Finally, there is the sun which

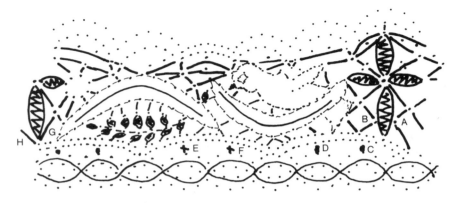

Pricking 27 This is one version of the crossroads footside. NB: Alternatives at A-B and G-H.

Plate 27 'Bicentenary'— Australia 1988

shines most of the time over people of all races, faiths, and human characteristics who have made Australia their home.

Materials: Approximately 24 prs of bobbins, wound in No. 90 linen lace thread or No. 30 DMC Retors d'Alsace cotton thread. This number of bobbins allows for them to be re-used after having been taken out of the work; extra will be needed if you intend to add a completely new pair each time.

To Work
See Fig. 9.9 for the working diagram.

Start with the footside; different versions of this type of footside occur in quite a few pieces of Bedfordshire lace, the main difference being in the method used in either crossing or linking the trail, using the crossroads method—i.e. a multi-crossing. As this footside does not have any recognised name I am calling it the 'crossroads footing' (or footside). Start at A, the final pin of the crossover, and work the trails down each side of the oval with 2 prs of passives and 1 pr of workers; either 1 or 2 twists at the pin and work a multi-crossing at the join between the 2 adjoining links of the chain. Add in 3 prs at C (for the narrow trails) and a further 4 prs at D where the first tally links with the narrow trail, and a plait starts.

The narrow trail
1. The narrow trail is worked in (wh. st.; twist) having 2 prs of passives, and the workers; sometimes it is increased in width, where prs join it, later to go out again; these additional prs are usually worked in plain wh. st., so that we prevent

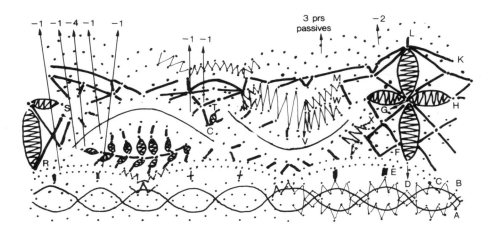

Fig. 9.9 Working diagram for 'Bicentenary'

the trail from becoming too wide. Join in 2 prs at E and start the lower tally of the cross; as this is a fairly long tally the shaping needs to be carefully watched. New prs are needed at F for a ground plait, the method used to add them in depending on how brave you are feeling! If very brave you can actually link the plait into the tally by taking the tally weaver and when you reach point F weaving it—yes, literally weaving it— through the 2 prs from its starting point to the right edge; pin; and weave it back again through the same 2 prs. If feeling less brave, you can take the plait from S to R (see the second cross in the pattern) down to the point where the lower tally of the cross started, linking it in there. If you are working the first method, the 2 prs from the plait will have to be carried either across the tally or worked in a small plait across the tally. Again, the decision is yours, but either method needs practice for a good result. Finish the tally to G and work the tally which goes from H to G. Work an 8-plait crossing, adding in 2 prs between the 2 tallies, then complete the cross.

The headside

7. Now turn to the headside, a simple Cluny-style heading, adding in 2 prs at each of the pins K and L; work plaits to the top of the tally, joining the 6 prs there with a 6-plait crossing. The two pairs from the tally work a short plait to go into

the heading, and the other 4 prs work plaits to the base of the heading and to point M, the tip of the dove's tail.

At this point I shall leave the detailed instructions and just look at individual features. You should have no problems in putting the various parts together, using the working diagram, Fig. 9.9, to help you.

8. The boomerang has a dividing twist down the centre, starting at about the fifth pin from the top. About half of this feature has to be worked before you can start the *dove's tail*. This is worked in half-stitch, starting at the point X on Fig. 9.9. Pairs are carried through the boomerang to be ready to work the *body* of the bird. This is started in two places—at the tip of the wing, and at the end of the rump; the two portions are linked together from W onwards, and joined together at V, thus for the rest of the bird you work straight across the rows. The boomerang and bird are linked together where they share a pin, working the 2 parts concurrently, and the bird is linked with the heading by plaits. The eye is a small hole—see Fig. 9.9.

9. The olive branch is a spray of leaf-shaped tallies, with short plaits leading into each tally as in the flower in 'Tassie'. Note that a tally was inadvertently omitted in the worked sample, Plate

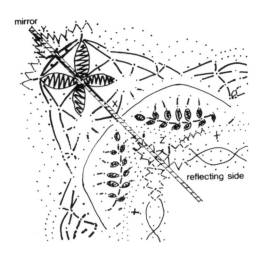

Fig. 9.10 Drawing a corner showing the position of the mirror, and adjustments to the pattern at Z, X and Y.
NB: This corner is 10% of the original pricking

27, (from T to U in Fig. 9.9), and was not picked up until the sample was taken from the pillow. It illustrates admirably how careful one must be in marking up a pricking, particularly when the work is dense, close or fine!

10. The *sun* is a half stitch bud.

That completes one pattern repeat. If you want a corner you should not find it difficult now to add one. Take a mirror and place it diagonally across the pattern as in Fig. 9.10. Move it, still on the diagonal, across the lace until you find a corner which pleases you; draw a diagonal line at this point on a spare pricking sheet (you are quite at liberty to take a photocopy of the drawing for your own use only—you will find 2 or 3 copies useful). Double check that it is the corner you want, then place the 2 footsides to meet at the common point. This will leave you with 2 portions of the corner and a gap in the centre which has to be filled in; this can either be drawn in freehand, using features from the main pattern, but possibly slightly changing their shape to fit the space to the best advantage, or you can trace actual features from the pattern, if you haven't the confidence at present to draw freehand. Plaits, tallies and kisses will be used to link the various parts, and fill in small gaps. The headside will need some adjustment to make it fit comfortably into the new shape.

The straight piece of lace could be put around the box or jar to make a lasting reminder of the place our craft held in this special year of Australia's bicentenary, and you could draw up a small motif (using perhaps the bird, the olive branch and the heading) for the top of the box. Just give it a little thought, and I am sure that ideas will come pouring in! If you worked a corner, a bicentenary mat is one of the obvious uses for the lace; again, you will think of many others.

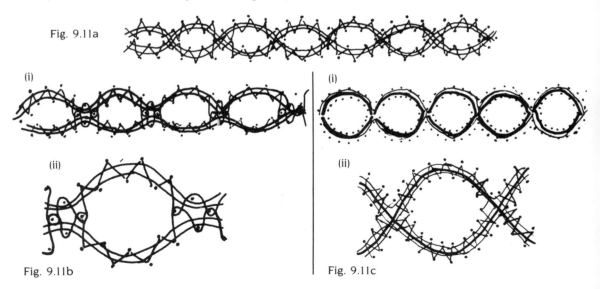

Fig. 9.11a

(i)

(ii)

Fig. 9.11b

(i)

(ii)

Fig. 9.11c

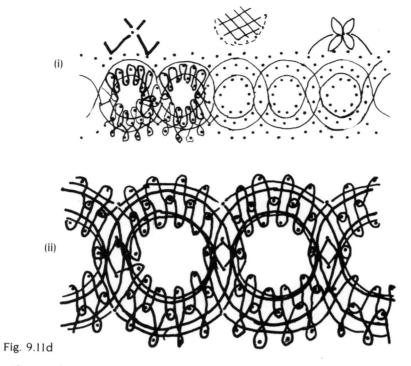

(i)

(ii)

Fig. 9.11d

Fig. 9.11 These are the four versions of the crossroads footside, with working diagrams of versions b, c and d. Fig. 9.11d(i) shows joins with other parts of the pattern

10 Mainly Maltese

The three pieces of lace in this chapter introduce us to the special techniques which occur in Maltese lace. Many, if not most, of my readers will be familiar with the ecru silk favoured by the Maltese lacemakers in the early years of this century, and many may even have the treasured piece carefully tucked away in a drawer or chest. Certainly there is a great deal of it around, particularly here in the Antipodes, and some of it may have reached these shores in as complex a way as my two special pieces of Maltese lace did.

I have tried to include as many of the special features of Maltese lace as possible, but one major one has been omitted; many of the old pieces of Maltese lace give the initial appearance of falling apart, but in fact they are made in strips, and joined together by a simple oversewing stitch, and it is *that* which breaks. Repairing the piece of lace is a comparatively simple job, the hardest part of it probably being the acquisition of a suitable thread. I have not used this technique here, although the very tatty round mat which was acquired in a literal junk shop for a few pence only, and which provided the inspiration for the square mat, was made in this way. Both the mat and the insertion in this chapter could easily be worked in portions (the mat) or strips (the insertion) and then joined up, but hopefully in a more secure manner than much of the earlier, true Maltese lace. A modern example of lace made in strips is the beautiful christening gown made by Josephine Caruana, a Maltese lacemaker who now lives in Sydney (Colour Plate 8).

These three patterns were named by the group of largely Maltese lacemakers of Parramatta, a suburb of Sydney.

Combine

The first piece we will work is the easiest, although some people may not think so with its large number of tallies! I must admit that it does look difficult, but in fact the only two prerequisites, in addition to your previous knowledge, are plenty of patience, and the ability to know when to call a temporary halt if you are tiring, as that is the time when tallies can easily go haywire and spoil the overall effect. The design uses features from two traditional collars; one had a very open footside and heading, which looked very untidy, and in the second the tallies were twice as close as in the arrangement I have used, and I did not think that this would necessarily be

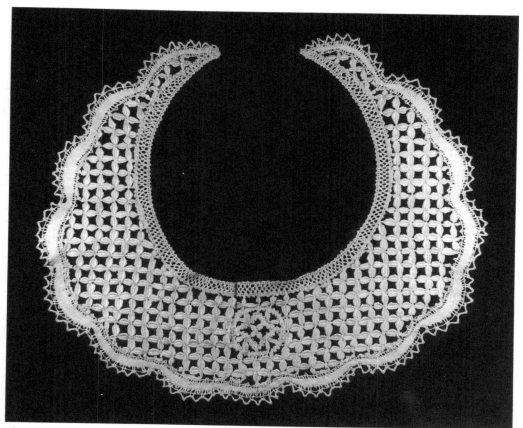

Plate 28a The Maltese collar

Plate 28b The centre back of the collar, showing the central motif

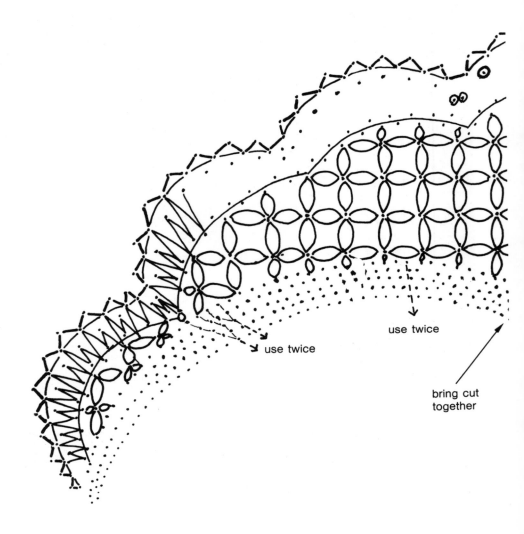

use twice

use twice

bring cut
together

Pricking 28 Bring the cuts together for the correct positioning of the pricking.

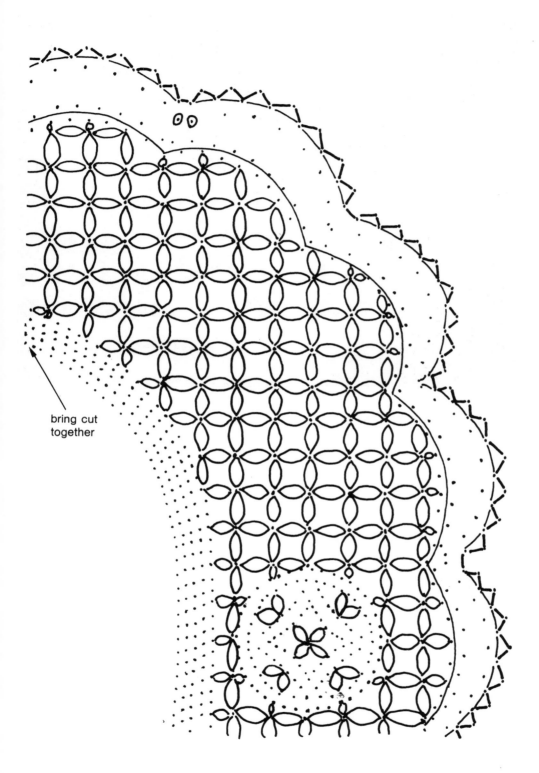

bring cut
together

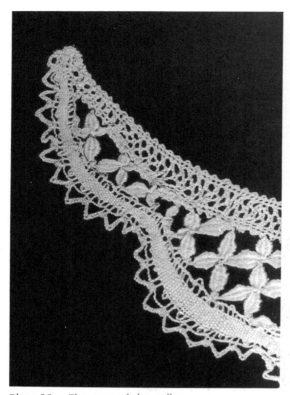

Plate 28c The start of the collar

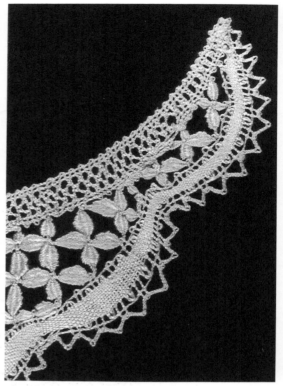

Plate 28d The ending of the collar

appreciated! In each of the collars the central motif was a Maltese cross, but again, I did not think that that was totally appropriate if the collar was to be worn by non-Maltese lacemakers, or their friends, all around the world!

Materials: A minimum of 40 prs of bobbins; thread equivalent to No. 70–80 linen. I particularly wanted a broken white (ecru) silk, but being unable to find any the correct colour and size I turned to a hank of silk I bought at a weavers' suppliers in a small country town in northern Victoria several years ago. The resulting collar is quite soft, but with a very attractive sheen, and is just what I wanted. This illustrates a very important point—don't be afraid to try almost any thread as long as it is not stretchy. This is a most important point: polyester thread and some cottons with a very strong twist are quite unsuitable for lacemaking, as they disappear to virtually nothing when the pins are removed, but otherwise do experiment; it is half the fun of putting your advanced knowledge into practice.

To Work

1. Following working diagram Fig. 10.1, start at the front point A with 6 prs. While the point is very narrow there is some deviation from the normal pattern, so start with the neckband (footside) and work straight wh. st. to E, adding in a further 2 prs at each of the pins C, D and E. At B add in 3 more prs to start the zig-zag plaited heading. This does not have a picot at the apex; the outer pr is just given 1–2 extra twists to go around the pin, and the plait is continued back to the link with the weaver. The continuous line inside the heading is a twisted pair of threads, the twists used being adjusted for each space; you will quickly fall into a pattern of the number of twists which you use, which will only need to be changed in places where the curve straightens out slightly—remember that a collar is not a true semi-circle.

2. Return to the footside and at E start pattern (a) for the footside. This is worked with 4 prs of passives and 2 prs of workers and is a simple

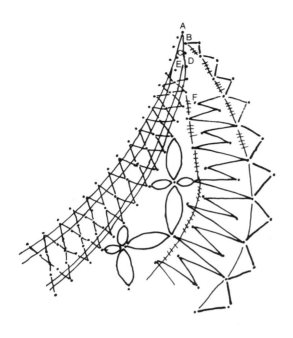

Fig. 10.1 The start of the collar

twisted footside with the workers meeting in the centre where they link with a (1/2 st.; twist; pin; 1/2 st.; twist). You will see where prs have to be added in for tallies so I need not mention them, but we will return to the start of the main headside trail. The pairs from B, as we have already seen, are used for the heading and the twisted inner pair. Of the pairs added in at C, D and E, the two prs added in at both D and E are not required for the footside so they can become 3 prs of passives and 1 pr of workers for the trail; 3 further prs are added in at F, 2 for trail passives and 1 for the inner edge twisted line.

3. The trail itself consists of alternating long and short rows, as can be most clearly seen in the working diagram, Fig. 10.1. One row works to the right and passes through the headside line (of twisted threads) to link with the plait from the heading, and then it works to the left, where the pin is inside the inner line, so this is not included in this, the short row. The next is a short row to the right, where the same applies, then we have a long row to the left where the workers pass (with a wh. st.) through the inner line; twist as many times as you decide, then keep to the same

number for this particular line of pin holes—which can vary from the number of twists you use to go around one of the inner pins if you so wish. Link a tally in to the weaving in the normal way; the majority work in and out at the same pin, but there are places where the 2 prs from the tally have to be carried along either in the footside, or in the headside trail. This causes no problems in the footside, but in the headside there is the line to be accommodated, which takes a bit of careful management if it is to remain intact and you are not to lose the spaces between it (the line) and the cloth work. I would suggest either carrying the pairs around on the inner edge inside the line until they are due to come out or weaving them right through to become part of the cloth work, but you will discover your own preferred way, which will quite likely be neither of these.

The footside

4. After you have worked the first tally of the second group the footside is wide enough to start pattern (b), the main part of the footside. This is not easy to describe, so I suggest you carefully study the working diagram, Fig. 10.2, and Plate 28c, to determine how to work it. Basically the two vertical rows of double stitch (whole stitch and a twist) continue as in part (a), so it is only the central crossings which are new. Two pairs are added in where part (b) of the footside starts, and are used to link with the workers on each side in (1/2 st.; pin; 1/2 st.), and then they link with each other in the centre. Once a rhythm is established there are no real problems unless you get out of step on the pricking, or the pricking is incorrect! I repeat, do study the working diagram carefully, and you should have no difficulties.

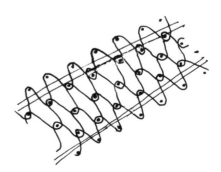

Fig. 10.2 The footside

The motif in the centre back

5. This is really quite simple. The circle is worked once again like that in 'Helianthus' (Chapter 2). There should be no need to repeat this by now, but I do so just in case! Two pairs come from the vertical tally directly above the centre of the circle, and the rest are added in at the start to work the diamond, making it as dense as you like. Similarly, pairs are added in, and later taken out, for the tallies between the circle and the diamond, and in the centre 'flower'. The workers of the diamond link with the outer circle at each of the corners, the first by adding in pairs, and the last by bringing the pairs out to work the equivalent vertical tally to that whose prs we used at the start of the circle. The workers of the circle and diamond link at the side corners.

To finish off

6. Gradually throw out pairs wherever your work gets thick, or where there is a suitable place to do so; remember that pairs can be 'lost' in the framework of a tally, and that after working one or two stitches after the tally, they can be just cut off. Try to get down to a maximum of 12 prs to avoid undue bulk at the end where threads have to be sewn in; remember that you started with just 4 prs, quickly adding in another 9 prs, and that looks quite bulky enough. The two ends should match as nearly as possible, particularly as they fall in the centre front of the dress, jumper or blouse on which the collar is mounted.

Notes

1. Where you have a very short tally linking either the footside or the trail with the normal sized ones, a plait can be used instead of the tally, and in some cases looks much neater. The difference barely shows.

2. The central motif can be used on its own as a small motif for a trinket box, key ring or brooch, but you may have to adjust the size of the pricking, probably by reducing it, and then working it in a finer thread, to fit into the mount.

Have fun! This collar is not really at all difficult to work, and I am sure that you will find that the end result justifies any little extra bit of effort, if only in the mind, that you have had to put into it!

Bizzilla

The central square is the only part of this pattern which should cause any problems, but the large areas of twisted interleaving threads need care in working to keep the mesh even.

Materials: Approximately 50 prs of bobbins, wound in No. 80 linen lace thread, or the equivalent cotton thread. This pattern does need a thread which gives a firm lace, otherwise the areas of twisted thread tend to curl slightly, especially the heading.

To Work

At this stage of the book I will only provide instructions for any parts of the pattern which are new, or which need special attention.

1. Start with the curved plait which forms the framework to the 9 tallies, the whole motif coming immediately after the corner—see working diagram, Fig. 10.3, if necessary. Hang 4 prs on a pin placed at A and work a plait to B where 2 more prs are added in. Continue this plait, adding in (and leaving out immediately) 2 prs at each of the pins C and D and 4 prs at E. Work the whole motif, either commencing the whole stitch band around the central square, and then joining in 2 prs for the central plait at G, or just hang these prs on a pin and take a sewing when you come to work the square later. The same point applies at H, so perhaps we had better start the square.

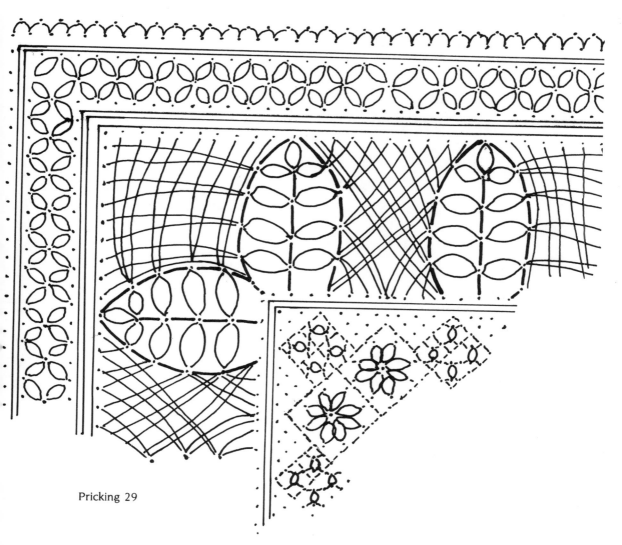

Pricking 29

2. Each of the diagonals is a plait, which occasionally acquires an additional pair, so start on the diagonal line nearest to the main starting place, and add in pairs all the way down the plait. The ground is torchon, as it is called by the Maltese, and the join with the outer rim of the square is also a torchon stitch. All the tallies start with one pair from each of two adjoining pin holes which are linked together with (half st.—or wh. st. if it holds the pairs together more satifactorily, pin; half or wh. st.). It is at the lower end of the group of 4 tallies that you may have an extra pair to be worked into the diagonal plaits. The central flowers should present no problems,

and the only other point to note is that in the centre of the rim there are two snatch pins.

The blocks of twisted interlinking threads
3. As already mentioned, great care has to be taken with tension here, otherwise there are difficulties. The number of twists between each wh. st. link depends on the distance that the twists have to cover, and you will find that you have to adjust this number on most occasions that you do a row of twists. You will notice that sometimes the pairs link directly in and out with the inner row of the edge pattern, and sometimes they stay in, ready to be used again at the next twisted block.

Plate 29 Square Maltese mat—'Bizzilla'

The heading portion

4. The inner square is slightly different from anything that we have done previously, so take a careful look at Fig. 10.3b. The tallies and double st. (wh. st.; twist) outer square should only need a reminder that each alternate 'join' links with the tallies, while there is a snatch pin at the intermediate pins. The exact headside is a row of zig-zag twisted loops (which just pass around a pin at the apex) and which link with the outer square in a torchon (half) stitch.

I found this mat slightly slow to work, largely due to the care which is needed with the large number of twisted threads, but I enjoyed doing it, and found it very rewarding—I hope you do too!

118

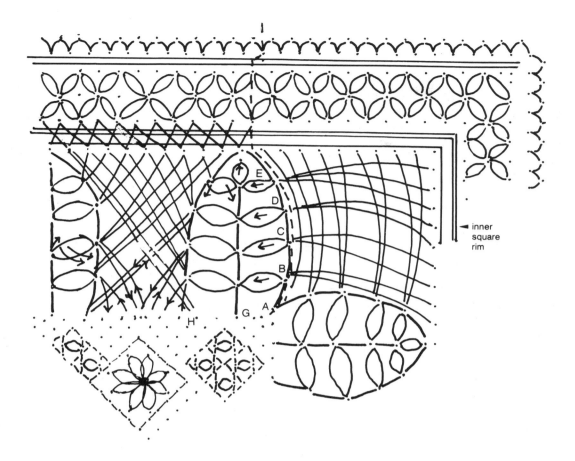

Fig. 10.3a Working diagram for the start and corner of 'Bizzilla'

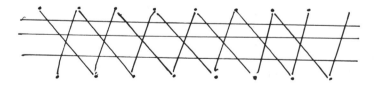

Fig. 10.3b Working diagram for the inner square rim

Olympia

This insertion includes three further Maltese techniques—the spider, worked differently from those that we are almost certainly familiar with; the Maltese cross; and the ground, which is called 'English ground'. As the pins in 'Olympia' are fairly close together, I would suggest that you work a Maltese cross, and a small portion of the ground, before starting the actual insertion. Josephine Caruana (see Foreword) has worked the cross as a small motif—an ideal gift for an expatriate Maltese when mounted in a trinket box or under a glass paperweight.

Materials: For the samples, use approximately 24 prs bobbins wound in a thickish thread, such as No. 40 or 50 linen thread. As these are only working samples you need not worry unduly about the exact size of thread, so here is an opportunity to use up any short lengths that you have left on your bobbins.

For the insertion 'Olympia', you need approximately 80 prs of bobbins, wound in No. 80 linen lace thread. I used the new Fresia Belgian linen lace thread, and found it to be a very even thread to work with. You will also find it a definite bonus to have an enlargement of the pricking, either to follow or to draw on.

To Work
A. The Maltese Cross
Referring to Fig. 10.4 and the working diagram, Fig. 10.5a, hang 8 prs from a pin placed in A, ensuring that 6 of the prs actually hang from one of the threads which will form the twisted outer rim. Twist the outer two pairs as many times as needed to reach B and C; put up pins to support the threads, or better still, do a half-stitch, with the two threads around each pin. Either work each of the three tallies (Maltese style of course!) or work a short plait before going into your tally; the choice is yours.

Turn to the r.h. side of the top quarter of the cross. Add in 2 prs at E (with a wh. st.), and as you are working, 1 pr at each of the pins G to

R inclusive. You will also be bringing in the prs from the tallies.

Starting at E, work a long row of wh. st. to X, including each of the prs hanging from the pins last mentioned; pin in X. *Work back to the end of the second row, leaving out pairs as shown in Pricking 30. **Continue each row as from * to ** until you arrive at the lower point with 2 prs left; these will join into one of the other portions of the cross.

The lower portion is worked as the upper but in reverse; it will be obvious where the work is divided, and each side is finished off independently, throwing out pairs if possible when the work gets sufficiently dense, and linking the points with the outer circle.

The side portions of the cross. Start the r.h. side at N and work *across* the v-shape; as before, work in reverse, bringing in pairs from the central ladder and also from the three tallies (which will be worked as shown in the working diagram, with 2 prs being added in to work the third tally). The pins on the inside of the V are snatch pins, except where the tallies are brought in or left out.

To finish off, sew all pairs back into the work, either into the centre of a tally, or into the points of the side and lower Vs or, very carefully, into the twisted circle, as has been done at the lower end of the ladders in the worked sample, Plate 30.

General notes
1. When working the side Vs, work the first half of each, then link the first three Vs by taking one of the side prs of workers and working in wh. st. over and back through all the prs you have—from the top lower point, the 2 ladders and the opposite side.

2. In some versions of the cross it is necessary to gain on a pin once, or even twice, in the centre of each of the sides' space. The pin can either be used twice (the most usual method), or you can change over the workers with a pr of passives.

3. In different versions of the cross we meet with varied numbers of pairs to be brought in for

Pricking 30

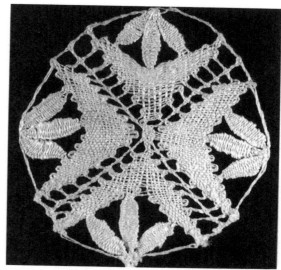

Plate 30　The Maltese cross

Fig. 10.4 The usual presentation of a Maltese cross pricking

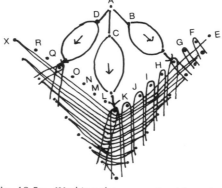

Fig. 10.5a Working the upper (and lower) portions of the Maltese cross

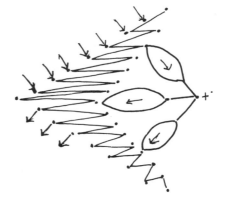

Note: The different positioning of the tallies in diagrams 10.5a and 10.5b—they are alternatives

Fig. 10.5b The side portion of the Maltese cross

Fig. 10.6 Pricking for English ground (enlarged)

working the first quarter, and thus varied numbers of pairs to go into the ladder between each of the quarters.

4. While perhaps not traditional, a plait could be worked around the edge instead of the twisted circle, making it all much stronger, particularly if this motif is going to be mounted and used. You could even go as far as to work a narrow trail in place of the twisted circle.

B. English Ground

Prepare a short length of pricking as in Fig. 10.6. As this is only a sample, the pricking could be photocopied, have a piece of ordinary cardboard placed behind it, and be covered with coloured transparent sticky-backed plastic, such as Contact or Fablon. Scraps of thread, already on bobbins, approximately No. 50 linen, or its equivalent, can be used for the sample.

To work hang bobbins on the pins as illustrated in the working diagram, Fig. 10.8. For the first couple of rows the footside will not be used, so hang the 4 prs of bobbins as indicated, on O.

There are three distinct rows to this pattern, although you may prefer to think of it as two, depending on how you are happiest working it.

1. *Starting at pin O where you have 4 prs of bobbins, take the r.h. one as your workers and work wh. st. to the left through 2 prs; put a pin under the workers—do *not* cover it at this stage— and work a wh. st. through the last (3rd) pr. You will now have 2 prs on either side of the pin**.

Twist the workers 4–5 times then repeat from * to ** across the row.

2. In this row, no pr is worked right across the row—each group of 3 prs which you have around a pin is complete in itself. #Take the l.h. pr—the

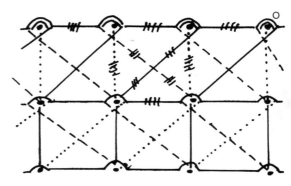

Fig. 10.7 Placing the pin in English ground

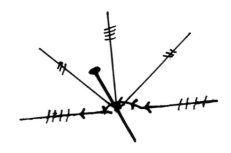

Fig. 10.8 Working diagram for English ground

single one to the l. of the pin—and work wh. st. through the other 2 prs, thus covering the pin.##

3. When 2 pins are up, you have the choice which gives you either 2 or 3 rows to the pattern. The r.h. pr from the l.h. pin, and the l.h. pr from the r.h. pin are each twisted twice, then worked together in a wh. st. with 2 twists to finish off the cross. This part of the ground can be worked as soon as you have 2 adjoining pins worked, or you can leave it until the end of the row and go right across the row, twisting the centre pr of the 3 on

each pin 4–5 times, and working each pr of crossed threads; I sometimes do one, and sometimes the other, but make sure never to muddle the two methods up, as I have found that one is in real trouble if one does. I still do not know which method I prefer.

At this stage it is unnecesary to worry about the ends of the rows—just make sure that you have 4 prs on the extreme r.h. pin so that you are ready to start the next row. Work as many as you need to, so that you feel quite sure of the pattern before putting it into the following insertion.

C. The Maltese Spider

As the other two new techniques have been learned, we will now look at the spider, then it is only a matter of putting them together to make the whole pattern. The spider occurs comparatively rarely in Maltese lace—in fact, I have only seen it once—but I am sure that this just a chance of fate in the pieces of lace which I have studied!

1. The spider is unusual in that the centre is a solid whole stitch block, so before working it I prefer to mark in, and then prick, the edge holes of the centre block (Fig. 10.9).

2. The legs are twisted as usual, and as there are 10 legs in all in each half of the spider, and the distance between the framework and the centre varies in length, it is a good idea to vary the

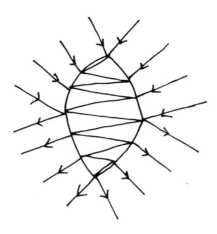

Fig. 10.9   The Maltese spider

number of twists. I suggest that you make a note of the number you have used for each leg to facilitate repeats.

3. The woven centre needs no explanation; start at the top where there are 2 prs and, working in wh. st., bring in and then, after the widest point, leave out, a pr at each pin hole. Finish off by twisting the legs as on the inward route, and then they will be worked into the framework at the appropriate time.

Good! We are now ready to start 'Olympia' (Pricking 31).

To Work

Hang pairs for the extended footside (which includes the tallies and trail inside them) with an additional 2 prs, which are used for linking the ground with the footside, on the inside pr of the inner trail. Three prs will be hung from each of the pins of the square grid with four prs (thus allowing for a worker pr) from the extreme r.h. grid pin. Look at working diagram, Fig. 10.9 again, this probably being much simpler to follow than the text at this point.

Having mastered the individual techniques the only tricky parts of the pattern now are the links between the inner footsides, the framework of the

spiders and the fitting of the Maltese cross into the ground. Obviously, as far as possible the ground is kept in its full form, but to fit with the parts mentioned above, some adjustments have to be made, and this necessitates the adding in and throwing out of some pairs of bobbins when joining the various parts of the pattern to make a whole. I am a bit reluctant to describe these links in detail as I have already worked them several different ways, and am sure that there must be even more which you, the readers, will discover, and which could well be infinitely neater than any of those I have tried. This was one of

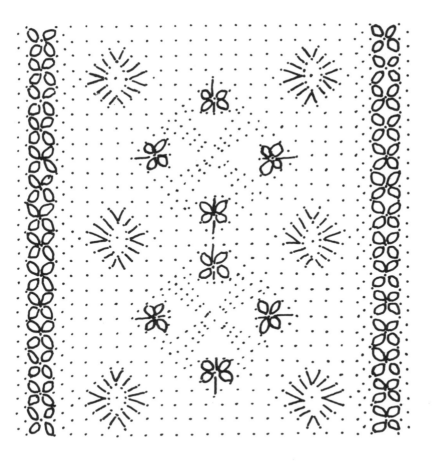

Plate 31 'Combine', showing alternative edgings for insertion; the Maltese cross; the Maltese spider and English ground

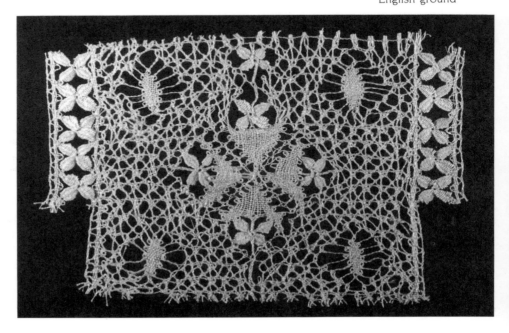

those patterns which, to start with, was more undone than done, largely because I was dissatisfied with these links!

There are, however, several points which have to be kept in mind.

1. When linking with the footside the r.h. pr from the first pin of the grid line forms the link with the inner pr of the inner footside, and then links with this first row of the grid.

2. On most rows one pr will need to be added in at this first grid pin but occasionally a second pr needs to be added in; these can be linked in when you are working or sewn in when you discover that an additional pr is needed.

It is *most* important that prs are added in here so that you can have the 2 prs of crossed threads, and the twisted thread which hangs vertically, thus keeping the pattern correct; the only places where the pattern may deviate slightly is around the crosses and the spiders.

3. There are points around the spider where you find yourself with either too many pairs, the number being, of course, determined by the number of spider's legs, or with too few. A pr can be thrown out in the centre of the pairs at each pin (after row 2 has been worked), or can be added in at a similar point, making sure that the 2 threads of the new pr become part of the two adjoining prs.

4. One pr for the starting point of the two upper tallies comes from the ground; it helps if you think of this point as being the crossed threads between the two vertical-lying threads on row 2 (or 3, if you have decided to think that way); one pr of threads goes to work the tally, with a second pr being added in, while the second pr completes the crossed threads of the diagonal.

The cross

5. It might be found helpful to join the outline pin holes of the cross, thus making it easier to see just where you are going. There are quite a few minor differences from the cross you have already worked; you will have the 2 prs at the top r.h. point to start with, but will need to add in prs at the next pin on the left, at the 2 'vacant' pins in the centre and at the penultimate pin on the left. On the side parts of the cross it is necessary to gain on a pin, using whichever method you like.

11 Gimp threads

Even an experienced lacemaker may not immediately think of gimp threads in the context of this family of laces, and yet they play a very important part in the more advanced pieces of Bedfordshire-Maltese and Cluny laces. Basically the gimps are used in two ways—as a continuous outlining thread, and as a thread which outlines part of the pattern only, thus creating the somewhat tedious job of finishing off after the gimp has done its outlining job, and starting again at the next pattern repeat. However tedious it might be, though, a gimp thread certainly adds that something to a piece of lace which makes all the working problems more than worthwhile.

Pam

As you might surmise, the first piece of lace we will make in this chapter features the continuous gimp thread; in the second the gimp just outlines the primrose flower, is finished off, and then is used again for the second and successive flowers.

Materials: 40 prs (approximately) of bobbins wound in Tanne (Madeira) No. 50 thread; 2 prs No. 8 pearl for the gimp threads.

To Work
Hang on bobbins as indicated on the working diagram, Fig. 11.1—a rough guide only—and work the footside (which has a snatch pin edge), the flower-centred braid ground, and start the horseshoe block—refer to Chapter 8, Figs. 8.1 and 8.3 if you have forgotten the ground.

1. The 6-petalled flower has already been worked in the pattern 'Tassie', Chapter 9; work petals 1, 2 and 3 of the flower, then turn to the Venetian

bar. Hang one extra pr at K, and work the Venetian bar up to L, using the pr from K as weavers, and taking these over and around 1 gimp pr on each side. At L let the bar weaver pass

Plate 32 'Pam'

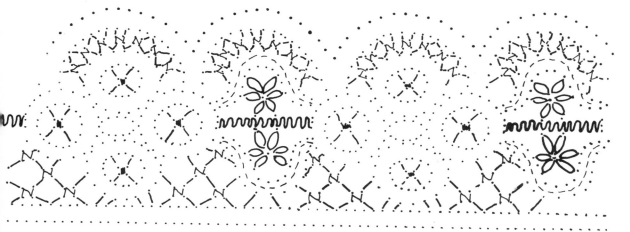

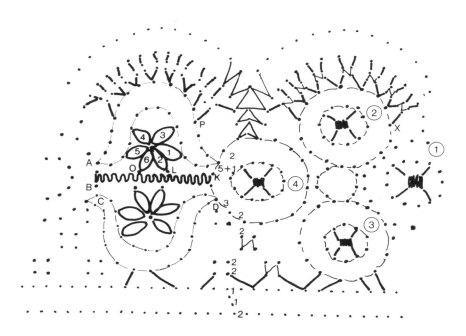

Fig. 11.1 Working diagram for 'Pam'

around it, then weave the 2 prs from petal 3 either together or singly over and under the passives of the Venetian bar to the left; they are now ready to work petal 2 of the l.h. flower. Continue weaving the bar until you reach O, then leave.

2. Turn to the l.h. horseshoe and work it and petals 1, 2 and 3 up to P where you join in 2 more prs with which you will work the linking filling—a slightly distorted flower-centred braid. Before you can do this you will have to start the headside trail, a basic whole stitch trail with a twisted edge pr and headside picots similar to the heading used in 'Hedgehog', Chapter 8, but here the picots are made by the main worker (weaver).

3. There should be no further problems until the headside, footside, two horseshoes, l.h. flower and

Fig. 11.2 The base of the headside trails in 'Pam'

ground have been worked up to O; here the 2 prs from petal 6 are worked through the Venetian bar, as you did at L, then all the parts mentioned above are completed up to the end of the horseshoes and of the bar. Having reached this point, you should have three prs remaining at the tip of each of the horseshoes, and 2 × 2 prs of gimps and 1 single working thread, both coming from the Venetian bar.

4. Add in one extra pr in the centre of the bar, i.e. between the two prs of gimp threads; these, and the pairs listed at the end of the last paragraph, are used to start the upper circle. Cross the two double gimps, r. over l., then bring the first two pairs of 'ordinary' threads, the weavers from the Venetian bar and the pair you have just added in, through the gimps, one on each side (tw. 1–2; gimp; twist); and then work these 2 prs through each other (in wh. st.), leaving them in these positions as the first pr of passives (a). See 'Jill', Chapter 6, if necessary. Bring in one pr from each of the pointed ends of the horseshoe on the r. and on the l. and work through passives (c). Passives (c) come from the 2nd pr at the bottom of the horseshoe; they are passed through the gimp on their respective sides, worked through passives (a) and (b) on each side, then worked (wh. st.; tw. × 2; pin in A (Fig. 11.1); wh. st.; twist). Leave as the inner pr of passives. Take the final prs (3) from each horseshoe as workers for their respective sides of the circle, and proceed as normal in a circle of this kind. You will find that Cluny crossings are worked wherever possible, for example where prs are left out for the plaits of the filling almost immediately, and also that the circle becomes very dense in places; you may therefore wish to throw out some pairs in the cloth work.

5. Do not forget that the gimp threads lie outside the pins of the main cloth work, and that plaits, etc. come in through the gimp, *then* are brought into the weaving. If the workers have to go out through the gimps they work through the passives; tw. × 1-2 times before and after putting up the pin, then through the gimp to do whatever they have to do. Coming back through the gimp, twist the same number of times as before it.

Circle no. 2
6. At A take the plait prs *in* to the circle through the gimp and link with the workers (rather than taking the workers out—this causes a 'bump in the gimp). In this, and in circle no. 3, you will need to add in prs, and in all four circles pairs will need to be thrown out when the work gets too dense, especially towards the end of each circle.

7. The headside trail should cause no further problems, but here again you may need to throw out prs if the cloth work gets too dense, especially where the work thickens at the base of the V of the trail. If you get into difficulties with this part of the pattern, refer to Fig. 11.2.

General reminder
1. Don't get too far ahead in any one part of the pattern; try to keep as near the horizontal at the conclusion of each portion as possible.

2. When gaining on a pin, by whatever method, make sure that you don't pull too tightly, otherwise a very marked hole can result.

3. If bringing in and leaving out pairs using the Cluny method of 'passing through the trail', you can use up an extra pin hole which may be causing you problems.

Primrose

This pattern introduces the second way in which gimps are used in this group of laces. We used an unbroken gimp in 'Pam', but here each flower is outlined in gimp which is then finished off and rejoined to start the next flower.

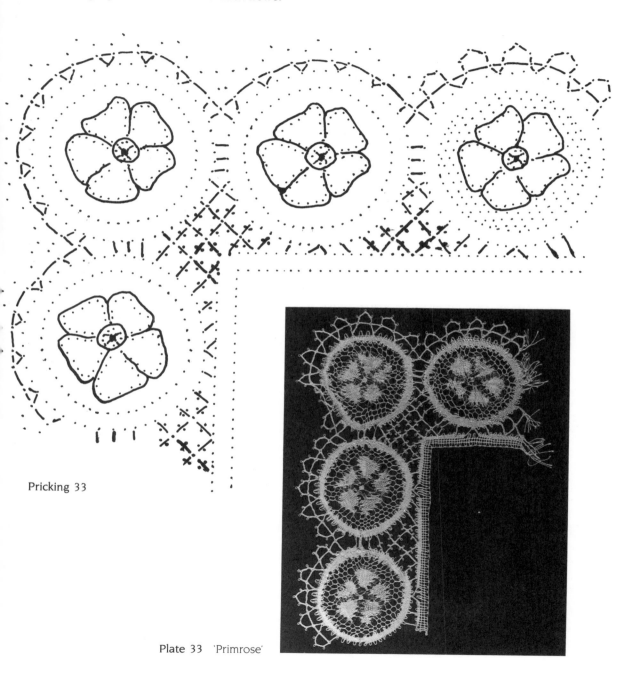

Pricking 33

Plate 33 'Primrose'

Materials: Approximately 45 prs of bobbins, which includes the extra prs you need for the corner; 1 pr of gimps plus a short length for each flower for the gimp for the centre—there is no need to wind this piece on a bobbin as it is so short. The sample (Plate 33) was worked in Zwicky 100/3 silk thread ('Iris'), in a primrose colour, and No. 8 pearl cotton in a leaf green was used for the gimps. Any equivalent linen or cotton thread can be used.

Preparation: Fill in the ground in all circles but the first.

To Work

Start the trail as you did for 'Helianthus' (Chapter 2), having 4 prs of passives, and work approximately 6 pins on each side. Prs will need to be added in on the inside where the filling links with the trail, and at the start, where the pairs from some of the plaits are brought into the trail. These plaits cross through the trail in a Cluny-style crossing if possible. Work the trail and filling to Y, where you will find that you can go no further until some work has been done on the petals.

Turning to the working diagram, Fig. 11.3, it is obvious that petal (a) must be worked first, so hang the gimps around the topmost pin and remember that the gimp lies outside the pins of the petal in these laces; the lines of the workers show one way of working in this pattern, but as long as you leave out prs to link any two adjoining petals, and to work the central tally (passing the latter through the short gimp), you can work the petals as you like. I would strongly advise you, though, to obtain an enlarged diagram and to fill it in as you are working, so that each pattern repeat is identical.

There are four points which need further clarification, otherwise by this stage you should be able to work the rest of this piece up to the corner.

1. At X work your usual V (or U) join, then continue to work in to the inner edge; bring in the pair from the point ground, then work back to X. Work a wh. st. with the pr which were the original workers and change places—the second workers go out in the plait to continue the heading, and the first workers go through the trail

to the inner pin, which is then put up. In this way you have gained on a pin.

2. At the end of the first petal a you will probably be left with two prs, depending on how you worked the petals. If this is the case, one goes into petal c, and the second is carried around with the circle gimp to come out for working again at S. This is a very useful technique if you find that you have pairs not needed immediately but fairly soon—just keep this 'spare' pr inside the circle gimp (or in other cases, the appropriate gimp) and take any relevant pairs through (the gimp plus one or more prs being carried around), either way.

3. When you reach the end of the final petal, (e), the gimps are crossed right over left, and are then woven back on themselves, as far as you can go. Where two gimps lie side by side there is no twist between them—the twist(s) come after the double gimp.

4. As you approach the end of the circle you will need to throw out some prs, so that you are left with 4-5 prs of bobbins on each side. Knot the 2-3 prs nearest to the inside of the circle (in reef knots using single threads from each side) and leave ends long enough to be sewn in. Cross the 4 outer prs (2 from each side), in whole st. and take these pairs on to the next circle in double plaits (see Fig. 11.4).

The corner

5. The footside corner: Work through to the hole before the corner; bring in 2 prs (to work the plait whose pairs eventually go in to the flower petal). Work back out to the footside edge and leave these workers to become passives.

6. Work the second pair from the straight edge through all the others, and again leave to become passives.

7. Take the inside pr (nearest to the ground plaits) out to the corner hole; add in 2 prs and work back to the original position.

8. Work your twisted passive through all the others and leave to go out.

9. Work the second twisted passive through all the others; pin in the first hole after the corner, then this pair becomes the workers for the main body of the footside.

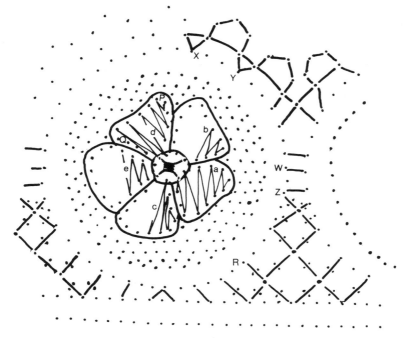

Fig. 11.3 Working diagram for 'Primrose'. NB: Pin holes for point ground not identical to pricking due to enlargement of the pattern

Fig. 11.4 The conclusion of each circle

The corner primrose and circle

10. Little explanation is required here, as the corner is worked very similarly to the main pattern. Petals a, b and c are quite straight-forward. Three pairs will probably need to be added between P and Q, 2 in the ground and one to go into petal d.

To work petal e give your pillow a quarter turn to the right; push down all the pins from the point ground, trail and nine-pin edging and cover this portion of your work with a working cloth, so that you have adequate space to work the

petal and are now working again in a normal direction, i.e. with your footside on the right. Finally, at or near the point R you will need to change the direction of the ground, working from the petal out to the circle.

'Stitches in the air'

There are places in this pattern where a great improvement is made if you fill in a large gap in the ground by working a 'stitch in the air'; unfortunately this is rarely obvious until you remove the pins, thus lending additional force to the oft-made suggestion that one should *always* work a sample, however small, before starting to work your final piece of lace.

To work a stitch in the air make an ordinary point ground stitch (1/2 st; twist × 2; pin) but do not put up a pin—for the very obvious reason that there is no pin hole there! When drawing up the ground one often finds that there is no room for any more pin holes but, as already said, one appears to be necessary; hence the use of yet another simple technique which can make a great difference to the appearance of your work.

12 Finale

The three pieces in this chapter bear no direct relationship to each other; they are merely grouped together, all being shapes of pieces of lace which we have not so far met.

The first piece, 'Julie', is a small oval which can be used for decorative purposes similar to the other motifs which have already been worked in this book. Alternatively, it can be used for dress purposes, such as a motif on a pocket, in the centre of a bodice, on a tie end—or indeed in any place you care to put it.

In the piece 'Bicentennial' you had a very slight introduction to the type of lace which Thomas Lester designed and made—although usually called Bedfordshire it contains features from both Honiton and point ground laces, and his work can only be described as exquisite. The fan leaf 'Autumn Leaves' carries this type of lace one step further, but is still only an introduction to Thomas Lester's style of lace.

The final pattern, 'Kowhai', features a beautiful New Zealand flower of that name, and I am most grateful to Irene Beck of Auckland for her drawing of the flower which forms the central feature of the triangle. Pieces of this shape are most useful for adding to an edging to create a more unified piece of work, such as on a tablecloth.

Julie

There is little which is new in this piece of lace, but one or two parts of the work need a little explanation.

Materials: Before starting, you will need to decide which sized motif you are going to work; that shown in Plate 5 is the largest and was worked in 50/2 Zwicky silk thread, Flora. The smaller of the 2 prickings given fits the oval paperweights, trinket boxes, etc., which are of English origin, but can be purchased from lace-suppliers or shops specialising in craft or embroidery in most countries where lace is widely made. You will need 18–20 prs of bobbins depending on the headside that you choose. For the smaller motif an assortment of silk threads, such as Zwicky Iris, No. 100/3; DMC Retors d'Alsace and Brillante d'Alsace, both No. 30, and Madeira Tanne, No. 30.

To Work
Firstly, choose which headside you wish to work: a straight edge (as in a plain footside); a snatch pin edge, as in the sample (Plate 34); a simple trail with a picot on the edge; a picot on a straight edge (as we have in Honiton lace).

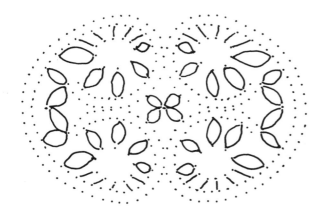

Pricking 34a 'Julie'—original size

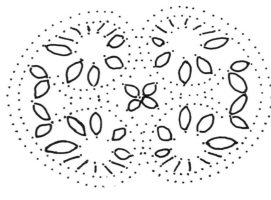

Pricking 34b 'Julie', reduced to fit oval trinket box

Plate 34   'Julie'

1. Following the working diagram, Fig. 12.1, start at A with 6 prs to give you 2 prs of workers and 4 prs of passives; use the circular start, as in 'Helianthus' and 'Primrose'. In some places the work will be sufficiently dense to leave out prs for the plaits and tallies which link the 'ring' with the centre of the flower, but in other places you will need to add in prs for these features. The flower centre looks best in half stitch, I think, but you can work it in whichever stitch you prefer.

2. When you have completed the flower centre and are bringing pairs back into the trail don't forget to start leaving them out as soon as your work is dense enough to hold the cut threads; this will depend to a large degree on the thread which you are using, as shiny silk obviously needs a greater density to support cut ends than matt linen does.

3. When you have completed the r.h. part of the trail you should aim to have 4–5 prs left (I needed 5 prs to hold the silk ends); work a normal tally with the l.h. 2 prs and a tally with 3 prs, doubling up the centre, support, pr on the r.h. tally. Note that trails 1 and 2 are linked on the sides with 4 kisses, so you will need to start trail 2 before you reach this point on trail 1.

4. You will notice that there is a little bar between tally 2 from the first quarter and 3 of the second quarter; this can either be a kiss (probably best in the smaller version of the pricking), or a sideways tally as in the sample shown here (Plate 34). Where the second quarter of the design

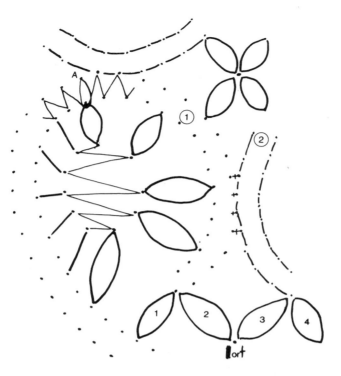

Fig. 12.1 Working diagram for the start of 'Julie'

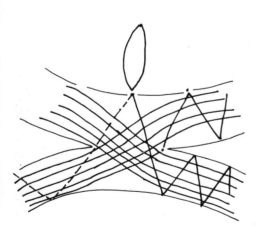

Fig. 12.2 The crossing between two adjoining trails (nos. 2 and 3)

adjoins the third quarter special treatment is needed; you have a tally on either side of the two trails, so take one pr from each of these and work wh. st. through their respective trails. The original workers become passives. Work a crossroads crossing with the 2 sets of threads, then find your original workers (from the tallies) and proceed in both directions along the outer trail of the third quarter. Fig. 12.2 will give you help if you need it with this crossing.

5. Work quarters 3 and 4, repeating any features from quarters 1 and 2 as appropriate.

To finish off

Work the crossroads crossing, or as much of it as you feel you need, or just take straight sewings into the starting holes (those that adjoin) of quarter 1, then finish off as usual, depending on the end use for your motif.

Autumn Leaves

I was travelling from London to Newton Abbot in Devon by coach when the idea for this fan leaf suddenly came to me—together with the idea of 'Primrose'—and I was so deep in my thoughts and initial scribbles that I nearly missed the stop, where my parents were waiting for me, after a two year absence! I am sure you will agree with me, however, that it was a very profitable journey.

Materials: I worked the fan in No. 80 linen lace thread—as usual you can make your own choice as the thread is approximately the same thickness.

You will also need a set of fan sticks, and this was designed to fit the small sticks—both plastic and wood—sold by the Springetts, of Rugby in the UK (see Appendix 2 for the exact address).

To Work

The headside is a slightly extended Cluny heading, and the footside is a cucumber foot. There are 2 grounds; in the outer portion, between the leaves and the heading, the ground is wh. st. apple blossom, while that in the inner portion, between the leaves and footside, is feather ground. Both these fillings/grounds were introduced in Chapter 8.

1. Now to the newer techniques (see Fig. 12.3); leaf (a) has raised tallies with square ends, some being worked across the leaf, and some being worked up and down the leaf, depending on the position of the tally. Work them as the raised petals in 'Lizzie', Chapter 7. The vein is a simple twisted line, which curves with the leaf.

2. The small gum leaf (b), is worked in whole stitch, and the larger gum leaf (c) has a twisted vein similar to that in leaf (a). The veins in leaf (d) are similar to kisses, with the workers from each side meeting and crossing with a wh. st. This leaf has no gimp, just a straight edge (a footside edge). When you are bringing in new prs in this leaf, I suggest that the Honiton method is used— work the row on which you intend to add a new pr; put up the edge pin (before working the change-over stitch—edge stitch), and hang the new pr around your workers, then lay them to the back of your work. Make up the change-over

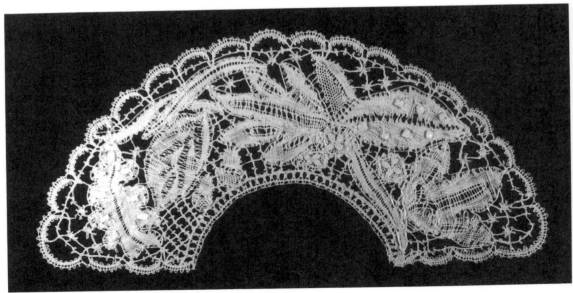

Plate 35 The unmounted fan leaf 'Autumn Leaves'

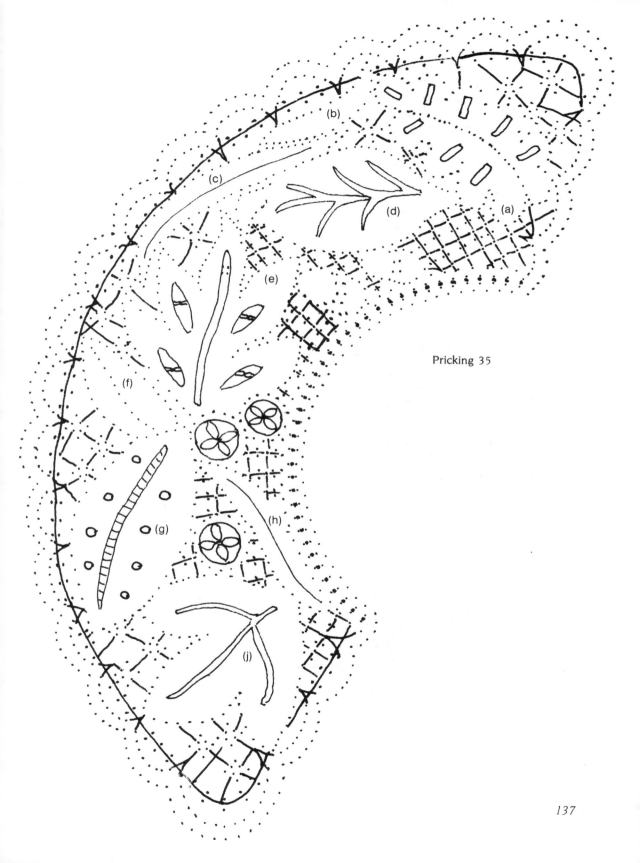

Pricking 35

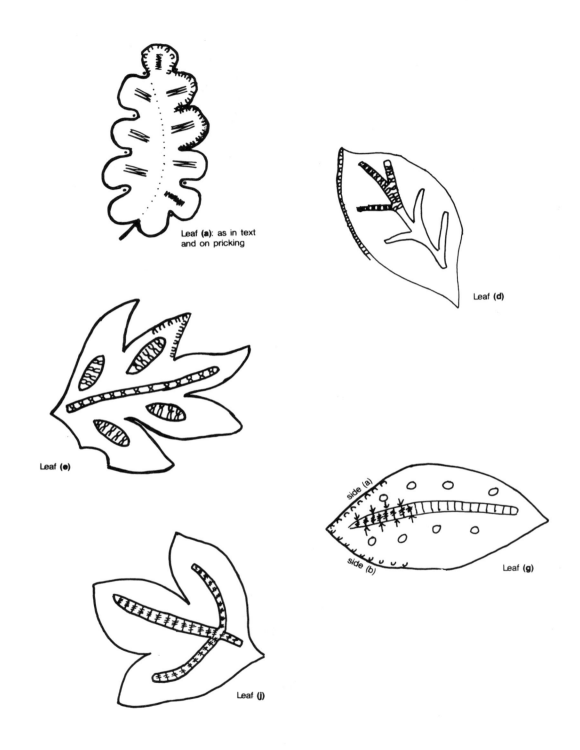

Leaf (a): as in text
and on pricking

Leaf (d)

Leaf (e)

side (a)

side (b)

Leaf (g)

Leaf (j)

Fig. 12.3 Leaves from the fan: for clarity the vein divisions and edge pin holes do not equate with those on the pricking

stitch then bring the new pr down into place just inside the change-over stitch; this is not a good place, though, to have a new pr as it breaks the edge line, so weave it through the first pr of passives so that it lies inside this pr. If you need to add in 2 prs at one place—never the best of ideas, but inevitable sometimes—add one before you work the change-over stitch, and one afterwards in the same way.

3. The acorns link with adjoining leaves so watch carefully to make sure that you do not get carried away when working leaf (d) and work beyond this link. The gimp only runs around the cup.

4. Leaf (e) has veins which are surrounded by gimps. The pin holes around the edge of the gimps are optional. In the vein, if you wish to transfer a pair from one side to the other, use a plait, otherwise use a kiss-style crossing.

5. The half-leaf (f) again has no gimp, and in this case the two sides, half and whole stitches, are linked at each row. Alternatively, if you are familiar with the methods of working, you can work this leaf as a Honiton leaf or a Bruges leaf.

6. Leaf (g) has bobble tallies, worked underneath the leaf, and single twisted threads carried from one side to the other forming the vein. In most cases the threads forming the vein are taken from side (a) to side (b), and then the next time they cross they are taken in reverse, from side (b) to side (a).

7. The final gum leaf (h) has a gimp, is worked in whole stitch and has a simple twisted vein. Adjoining this leaf are three gumnuts, which I worked in half stitch with three crossed raised tallies on top, as in 'Connie' (Chapter 8). Those who are familiar with gumnuts will know that the blue gum has a very clearly marked cross on it.

8. Finally, we come to leaf (j). I worked this in a very thin manner, wanting to get some contrast in the actual leaves between this and the other leaves, but you may prefer to add in additional pairs to thicken it up. The leaf has a gimp, and the veins are surrounded by gimps, with clearly defined pin holes outside the gimps (additional twists!) and, particularly in the centre lobe of the leaf, longer twists than those in the other leaves which I have worked in this fan.

9. Finish off as usual, by reducing the number of threads, tying off, and sewing the remaining ends into your work.

I wonder if you are thinking to yourself, 'This is all very personal'. Yes, I know it is, but this chapter is written deliberately in this manner. When we reach laces of this type, I feel that their working *is* a very personal matter; in addition, if you have systematically worked through the book you should have a good general knowledge of this family of laces, and it is not up to me at this stage to dictate to you just how you will work a piece of lace. Remember that there are many different ways of working most laces, and my philosophy is that the only correct one is that which pleases *you*, as long as you are maintaining the pattern which was designed in a particular way, and either keeping true to the type of lace, or making it quite clear that you are breaking away from the traditional way of working these laces.

Kowhai

And so we come to the final piece of lace in this book; now you can see how much you have learnt!

The only text you have is Pricking 36. It is not a difficult piece of lace, and a hint is given to you in the title, the name of one of the most beautiful New Zealand flowers, which bursts forth in its golden beauty shortly before Christmas each year. I would advise you not to try to keep to any one of the laces in this family, but to think of it as just a guipure lace, using features from each of the laces in this family.

It is my sincere hope that you enjoy this challenge and feel it a fitting close to this course

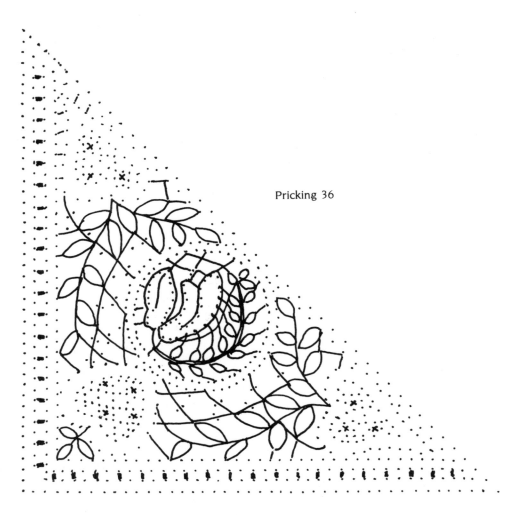

Pricking 36

in a modern approach to the Bedfordshire family of laces.

There are literally hundreds of traditional patterns waiting for you to enjoy in each of these laces, and I am sure that most of my readers will soon be designing their own lace using the techniques learnt in this book, if you are not doing so already.

Have fun, and good lacemaking!

Appendix 1—Thread Chart

(showing threads of approximately the same thickness)

I am using the Bouc (belgium) linen lace thread as the basic thread, and relating all others to that sizing. Do remember that there is considerably more give in threads used for making all three laces considered in this book than in a straight lace such as Point Ground, so my equivalents should only be taken as approximations.

Bouc linen: 30

Bockens linen (Swedish) No. 40/2; Campbells linen No. 60; DMC Cordonnet No. 40/50; Brok cotton No. 24/3.

Bouc linen: 50

Bockens linen No. 50/2; Campbells linen No. 70; Fresia linen (Belgian, new) No. 40/2; DMC Cordonnet No. 60; Brok 36/3.

Bouc linen: 60

Bockens linen 80/2; Campbells linen No. 100; DMC Cordonnet No. 70; Molnylcke cotton quilting thread; Mettler 40/3—these last two are between 60 and 80

Bouc linen: 80

Bockens linen 90/2–100/2; DMC Cordonnet No. 100 (slightly on the thick side); DMC Brillante d'Alsace and Retors d'Alsace No. 30; Zwicky Flora silk; Guterman silk No. 100/3 (slightly on the coarse side); Brok 36/2; Fresia No. 80/2

Bouc linen: 100/2

Bockens linen No. 120; Zwicky darning thread—reverse twist 70/2 (120); Fresia 100/2; Zwicky Iris silk No. 100/3—again, slightly on the thick side, nearer 90/2); Brok No. 60/2

Do remember that these are by no means the only threads suitable for making the guipure laces, as already mentioned (p.114). Don't be afraid to try *any* cotton or silk thread—or linen if you can get it—but *do* make a small sample of your pattern using the chosen thread to make sure that it is suitable for both the pattern and for you. Individual tension, preferences and expectations of the finished lace will all be different for individual lacemakers; you must find the thread which is best for you for each piece of lace that you make—and don't be afraid to alter the threads which I used when working the samples of each chapter.

Appendix 2—Suppliers of Lacemaking Equipment

Today there are literally hundreds of suppliers in countries all round the world, and it would be impossible to list them all; my apologies to those I have omitted. I have just picked representatives from English-speaking countries where there are Lacemakers who are most likely to use this book.

Australia

Randwick Arts and Crafts, 201 Avoca St, Randwick NSW 2031

Lacemaker, 724a Riversdale Rd, Camberwell, Victoria 3124

Dentelles Lace Supplies, 39 Lang Terrace, Northgate, Brisbane, Queensland 4013

Class Craft, 92 Unley Rd, Unley, South Australia 5061

New Zealand

Peter McLeavey, PO Box 69007, Auckland 8, New Zealand

United Kingdom

D.J. Hornsby, 149 High Street, Burton Latimer, Kettering, Northans

A. Sells, 49 Pedley Lane, Clifton, Shefford, Bedfordshire

Sebalace, Waterloo Mill, Howden Road, Silsden, West Yorkshire

Christine and David Springett, 21 Hillmorton Road, Rugby, Warwickshire

United States of America

Robin and Russ Handweavers, 533 N. Adams St, McMinnville, Oregon 97128

Lacis, 2150 Stuart Street, Berkeley, California 94703

Further information including addresses of further suppliers, can be obtained from the following National Organisations:

> The Australian Lace Guild
> The New Zealand Lace Society
> The International Old Lacers Inc. (USA)
> The Lace Guild (UK), The Hollies, 53 Audnam, Stourbridge, West Midlands DY8 4AE
> Kantcentrum, Balstraat 14, 8000 Brugge, Belgium
> Centre d'Initiation à Le Puy, 2 rue Duguesclin, 4300 Le Puy, France

As the first three of these organisations do not have permanent premises, I have not given any address for them, but they can readily be obtained through the relevant national craft coordinating body.

Bibliography

History and background knowledge
Bobbin Lace in Photographs—Voysey
Lace and Lace-making—Bullock
La Dentelle du Puy—une tradition—Jean Arsac
La Dentelle du Puy des origines a nos jours—Arsac
Pillow Lace in the East Midlands—Freeman
The Lavendon Collection of Bobbin Lace—Harris
The Romance of the Lace Pillow—Thomas Wright
Thomas Lester; his Lace and the East Midlands Lace Industry—Buck

Technical manuals
A Manual of Bedfordshire Lace—Pam Robinson
Bedfordshire Lace Patterns—Margaret Turner
Pillow Lace bks. 1 and 2—Hamer
Traditional Bedfordshire Lace—Barbara Underwood
Bobbin Lace—Le Puy style (part only)—Fouriscot, etc.
The Technique and Design of Cluny Lace—Paulis/Rutgers

Chapters and sections on Bedfordshire lace in the following books, to name but a few:

A Manual of Bobbin Lace Work—Maidment
The Dryad Book of Bobbin Lace—Rae Clare
The Technique of Bobbin Lace—Nottingham

Periodicals
Lace (The Journal of the Lace Guild, UK)—for patterns and the occasional article about history/background interest.

Patterns only
In the folders from Le Puy, especially catalogue B1, but some designs in most of the catalogues. Probably the best source of Cluny patterns is the quarterly French journal *La Dentelle*. Although it is in French, non-linguists should have no difficulty in following the very clear diagrams and photographs. *Kant*, published by the lace school, Bruges, also has Cluny patterns from time to time.

There is a dearth of printed material about Maltese lace; about all that appears in print are a few odd paragraphs on the history of the lace, and the structure of the tallies (wheatears), etc. Most knowledge has to be gained from studying old pieces of lace and photographs, or from conversations with Maltese lacemakers themselves.

Index

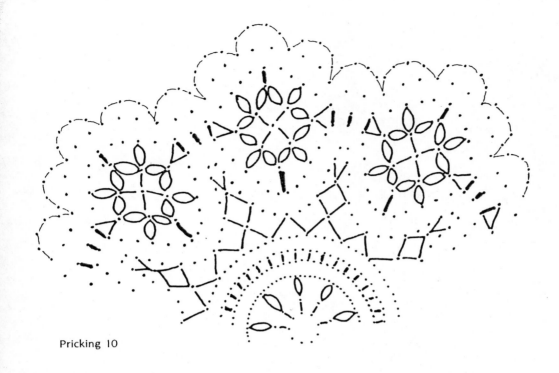

Pricking 10

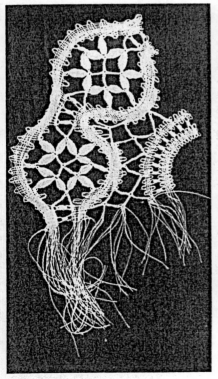

Plate 10b 'Venus', with a looped picot edge

Plate 10a A portion of 'Venus', with a straight edge

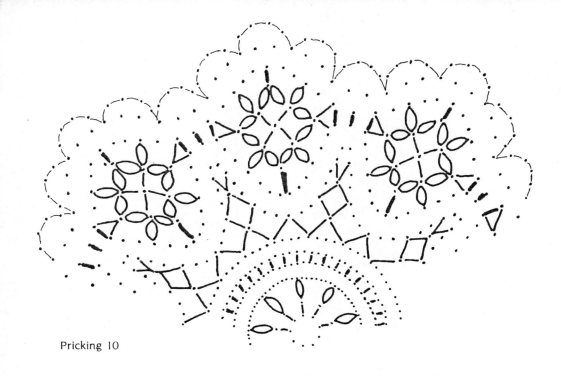

Pricking 10

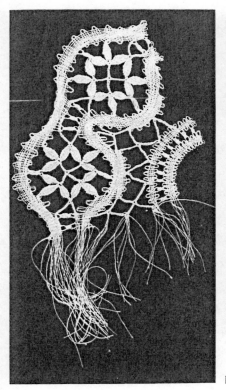

Plate 10b 'Venus', with a looped picot edge

Plate 10a A portion of 'Venus', with a straight edge